CHRISTIAN PRIESTHOOD

CHRISTIAN PRIESTHOOD

BY

HENRY BALMFORTH

Chancellor of Exeter Cathedral

LONDON

S · P · C · K

1963

First published in 1963
by S.P.C.K
Holy Trinity Church
Marylebone Road
London N.W.1

Printed in Great Britain by
Spottiswoode, Ballantyne & Co. Ltd., London and Colchester

NOTE

Part I first appeared under
the title *The Royal Priesthood*
in the "Beacon Books" series
of the Church Union in 1956

CONTENTS

PREFACE

There are many books dealing with the spiritual life of the clergy and there are others that discuss the theological foundations of priesthood. In the following pages I have attempted to treat these two themes as parts of a single whole, and to see the vocation of the clergy in its essential relation to the biblical data and to the faith of the Church. Accordingly, the first part is a brief study of the theology of priesthood in its threefold nature: its archetype in the creative and unique priesthood of Christ and the derivative and dependent extensions of priesthood in the Body of Christ and in the apostolic ministry. The second part— since this is a book addressed primarily *ad clerum*—considers the spiritual discipline and objectives of those who are ordained to the ministerial priesthood and are entrusted with the priestly ministry of the Word and Sacraments within the priestly Body.

No one can write a book about the Christian ministry to-day without being aware that in the ecumenical dialogue on reunion the ministry is one of the outstanding problems, still in need of much patient study. There are signs of a growing realization that those who discuss this problem must come to grips with the idea of priesthood, if a solution is to be found. We have heard much about episcopacy. We have heard much less about priesthood. Yet it may be suggested that, to say the least of it, priesthood is no less deeply embedded in biblical thought. Episcopacy, moreover, is sometimes presented as though it existed in a kind of theological vacuum and could be considered in isolation from its context in that historic threefold ministry which has come down to us from at least the beginning of the second century of our era. There is abundant evidence that this context includes the concepts of priesthood and sacrifice as implicit in the ministry of bishops and presbyters. This being so, we are bound to look again at priesthood and to rescue it from the polemics of four hundred years of ecclesiastical controversy. Priesthood has to be seen anew in the light of contemporary biblical, patristic, and liturgical study, to be rediscovered for what I dare to think it truly is, an indispensable part of the common Christian heritage, catholic and evangelical in the best sense of these terms. In this book I have sought to keep these considerations in mind and to present an "image" of ministerial priesthood, both theological and practical, which is faithful both to the Scriptures and to "what the Spirit saith to the churches".

The first Part of this book is a new edition, with only minor changes, of an earlier work of mine entitled *The Royal Priesthood*, first published in 1956 by the Church Union as a Lent book. Since the original edition is now exhausted, and the demand for copies still continues, this essay is now represented as a survey of the theological grounds upon which the ministerial priesthood rests. The second Part of the present volume is based upon a series of articles written at the request of the then Editor of the *Church Times* and published in that journal. For the present purpose these articles have been largely rewritten. I am indebted to the Church Union and to the proprietors of the *Church Times* for their consent to the use here made of this material.

PART I

The Royal Priesthood

1

THE PRIESTHOOD OF CHRIST

1

Priesthood has been one of the most controversial subjects in Christian history for the last four hundred years. In this book I wish to stand aside from ecclesiastical wrangling about it and consider it afresh in the light of the Bible. The reason for doing so had better be stated at the outset.

However it may have been used or misused, priesthood is an essential category for our understanding of the biblical revelation, and so for the spiritual life and welfare of the Christian. This is true not only of the Old Testament Scriptures; it applies also to the New Testament which rests upon the Old Testament for so much that is structural in its thought. If we are to understand Jesus Christ and the Christian religion with the help of the Scriptures—and all Christians agree that we must do that—sooner or later we have to come to terms with priesthood. Nor is this a merely theoretical concern, a matter that can be left to theologians in their efforts to formulate the Christian verity in its fullness. It is practical as well; for one of the most urgent needs of our time is that the Christian folk should realize in life and action that they are what a New Testament writer calls them, "a holy priesthood to offer up spiritual sacrifices".[1] To know Jesus Christ is to know him as,

[1] 1 Pet. 2. 5.

among other things, our great High Priest.[1] To know what
it means to be a Christian is to know oneself as sharing in a
royal priesthood.[2] And, if Christ is priestly and his Christians
priestly, it will be hard indeed to escape the further truth
that Christ's apostolic ministers are priestly.[3]

Priesthood and sacrifice: the terms belong to the religious
quest of mankind throughout recorded history, as well as
to the divine revelation uniquely made through Israel and
the Incarnate Word of God. They tell us of man's gropings
after God, and they tell us of Calvary. We shall not understand Maundy Thursday or Good Friday without them.
And it is equally true that we shall not find their full
meaning except by way of Maundy Thursday and Good
Friday. For the Christian understanding of priesthood rests
upon the unique and creative priesthood of Jesus Christ.
That is where we have to begin, with him in whom all the
shadowy and preparatory anticipations, even in Israel, are
set aside and the full, proper meaning of priesthood is
concretely exposed. Pre-Christian priesthood is but a
provisional foreshadowing of the real thing. Christian
priesthood, both the corporate priesthood of the Church and
the ministerial priesthood of bishop and presbyter, is
derivative and dependent. Priesthood in its fullness belongs
to Jesus Christ alone.

The priesthood of Christ, as the biblical revelation
declares it, would need a large, separate volume for any
adequate presentation. Here we must be content with a
more modest programme and confine ourselves to two lines
of inquiry. Our first concern is with Christ's priesthood, as
it is presented in the gospel material. Secondly we can seek

---

[1] Heb. 4. 14.   [2] 1 Pet. 2. 9.
[3] Cf. Rom. 15. 16 and C. H. Dodd's commentary (Moffatt series)
ad loc.

further help by drawing upon the argument of the Epistle to the Hebrews.

2

The gospel material is commonly supposed to fall into two main categories, the synoptic tradition of Matthew, Mark, and Luke, and that inspired commentary upon the words and works of Jesus which we know as the Gospel according to St John. This fourth gospel is not only a gospel in its own right, it is also far and away the best exposition in existence of the true meaning of the gospel story. If we want to know what the written records of our Lord's earthly life and ministry mean, the fourth gospel gives us at once the most authoritative and the most searching and profound explanation. Nowhere does this come out with more impressiveness than in John 17, the culmination of those marvellous chapters in which the meaning of the Lord's passion is set forth.

In John 17 we are told that the Lord, at the supreme moment of his earthly life, consecrated himself as the sacrificial victim.[1] That is the meaning of his death. He had himself declared it to be so by his acts and words at the Last Supper, when he instituted the Eucharist. What lies behind this self-consecration of the Messiah? Why was it necessary and what is it for?

To understand we must go a long way back in the sacred history, to the prophetic religion of the Old Testament.

From Amos onwards the prophets of Israel, as is well known, show a persistent uneasiness about the religion of God's people. On the one hand, they are utterly convinced that Israel is chosen of God to be his "peculiar people",

---

[1] John 17. 19. The Greek word *hagiazein* means "dedicate as a sacrifice"; see the commentary of Hoskyns and Davey, *ad loc*.

to love and serve him in a true and acceptable worship, and
—though this appears only in the highest moments of
prophetic vision—to be his missionary people to the Gentiles.
Thus Isaiah speaks for all the prophets when he says:

The vineyard of the Lord of hosts is the house of Israel, and the
men of Judah his pleasant plant. (Isa. 5. 7.)

The responsibility which goes with this position of privilege
is memorably stated by two later writers:

It is too light a thing that thou shouldest be my servant to raise up
the tribes of Jacob, and to restore the preserved of Israel: I will
also give thee for a light to the Gentiles, that thou mayest be my
salvation unto the end of the earth. (Isa. 49. 6.)

In those days it shall come to pass, that ten men shall take hold,
out of all the languages of the nations, shall even take hold of the
skirt of him that is a Jew saying, We will go with you, for we have
heard that God is with you. (Zech. 8. 23.)

The moral of the charming adventure story which we
know as the Book of Jonah is the same. Israel as a whole
may indeed be a backsliding and a faithless people, but the
faithful remnant will abide to carry on God's purpose,
which cannot fail.

Yet, on the other hand, the prophets are uneasy; and in
particular they are uneasy about the sacrificial worship
which was the centre of the national religion. Amos, the
earliest of the writing prophets, is uncompromisingly blunt:

I hate, I despise your feasts, and I will take no delight in your
solemn assemblies. Yea, though ye offer me your burnt offerings
and meat offerings, I will not accept them: neither will I regard
the peace offerings of your fat beasts. (Amos 5. 21, 22.)

So, too, Isaiah:

To what purpose is the multitude of your sacrifices unto me?
saith the Lord: I am full of the burnt offerings of rams, and the

fat of fed beasts; and I delight not in the blood of bullocks, or of lambs, or of he-goats. When ye come to appear before me, who hath required this at your hand, to trample my courts? Bring no more vain oblations; incense is an abomination unto me; new moon and sabbath, the calling of assemblies,—I cannot away with iniquity and the solemn meeting. (Isa. 1. 11–13.)

The prophetic movement itself had been responsible for the reform (mirrored in Deuteronomy) which set up the one central shrine of Israel's worship in Zion. But that purification of the older, contaminated worship did not satisfy, and we find the attacks on the sacrificial system renewed by Jeremiah.

I spake not unto your fathers, nor commanded them in the day that I brought them out of the land of Egypt, concerning burnt offerings or sacrifices: but this thing I commanded them, saying, Hearken unto my voice, and I will be your God, and ye shall be my people. (Jer. 7. 22.)

Sometimes the prophetic attack is clearly provoked by a grievous misuse of sacrifice and directed against the abuses and perversions which made ritual and ceremonial acts a mere substitute for a life ruled by the principles of justice and mercy. It has frequently been held that this suffices to explain the prophets' language and that they do not go further and question the sacrificial system as such. Yet it is difficult to stop at that point. The prophets do sometimes seem to want more than a simple correction of wrong attitudes to sacrifice. To judge from the strength of their downright language, they almost despaired of the whole system and questioned whether men could ever truly worship God in this way. In the sacrifices men give their possessions to God. It is possible, even probable, that the giver felt himself to be in some sense identified with the gift, so that he was, as it were, giving himself into God's hands. But, the prophets seem to ask, is this partial and limited method of self-oblation, even when it is genuinely felt and intended, good enough? Must we not go further and say, "not by anything that man *has*, but by all that man *is*, must God be worshipped"?

Now it is just at this point in the development of the prophetic insights that we discern, rising out of the sea of their perplexity and doubt, the mysterious, arresting figure of the Servant of the Lord, supremely depicted in Isaiah 53, but visible also in some of the psalms.

> Sacrifice and offering thou hast no delight in;
> Mine ears hast thou opened:
> Burnt offering and sin offering hast thou not
>   required.
> Then said I, Lo, I am come;
> In the roll of the book it is written of me:
> I delight to do thy will, O my God:
> Yea, thy law is within my heart.
>
> (Ps. 40. 6–8.)

> Create in me a clean heart, O God:
> And renew a right spirit within me . . .
> Then will I teach transgressors thy ways;
> And sinners shall be converted unto thee . . .
> For thou delightest not in sacrifice; else would I
>   give it:
> Thou hast no pleasure in burnt offering.
> The sacrifices of God are a broken spirit:
> A broken and a contrite heart, O God, thou
>   wilt not despise.
>
> (Ps. 51. 10, 13, 16, 17.)

In such passages and in the servant songs of the Book of Isaiah a new hope dawns. If only we could have *that*—so the prophetic movement in the end seems to realize—then Israel would be really Israel, really the servant and wor-

shipper of God. The Old Testament presents us with what
we may call a progressive concentration of meaning in the
image, or figure, of God's elect. First, it is the chosen people;
then it is the remnant; finally it is the Servant. Such, stage
by stage, seems to be the sequence of the prophets' thoughts
about God's overruling of Hebrew history and religion.[1]

Christianity, considered as a revelation through history,
may be said to consist in the affirmation that this wistful
"If only . . ." of the prophets of Israel has been given actual
realization in Jesus Christ. Whether or not the prophets
consciously perceived the bearing of their thought does not
affect the point. Jesus Christ *is* the true Israelite and the
Suffering Servant. He is the only true Israelite there has
ever been. For he alone has given that perfect filial obedience for which, ideally, Israel was called. God's purpose
in the call of his servant Israel did not fail, but it came to
fulfilment in a strange and tragic way. At one moment in
history the Israel of God dwindled to a single Man, and he
was dying on the cross, to which the blindness of priests,
scribes, and populace had consigned him. But out of his
uncompromising and perfect obedience, expressed in total
self-sacrifice, a wholly voluntary self-giving "even unto
death", there was born the New Israel, redeemed humanity,
the universal Church. So it is that, being himself the one
true offerer of the one perfect oblation, he makes possible
for his followers a share in that oblation and access to that
worship which St Paul was to describe as "a living sacrifice,
holy, acceptable to God, which is your reasonable worship".[2]

The gospel story, as the synoptic tradition and, most
vividly, the Gospel according to Mark, present it to us,

---

[1] See further on this subject Louis Bouyer, *Le Mystère Pascal*, pp. 273ff
(Eng. trans., *The Paschal Mystery*).
[2] Rom. 12. 1.

2

shows how Christ fulfils the hope of Israel in a bewildering and wholly unexpected way. It is this way of the Suffering Servant of the Lord. The ideal figure of Isaiah 53 comes to life in the passion of our Lord. His cross, endured, as St Mark insists, in complete isolation, is the supreme and central mystery in the whole amazing story of his earthly career. To the Jews a stumbling-block, to the Greeks foolishness, the cross is really, as St John says, his glory— "now is the son of man glorified"—at the moment when Judas goes out to set in motion the machinery which will bring the Lord to Calvary. It is also his victory: as he himself says, "I have overcome the world". And it is the priestly consecration of himself for the redemption of mankind, the climax and crown of that self-dedication to the Father's good pleasure which makes his death a ransom for many, "for their sakes I consecrate myself". He was both the priest and the sacrifice. He came to do the will of him that sent him and he fulfilled his mission to the end. Nothing was held back. Whatever man's sin laid upon him he would bear. The surrender is total and the offering the greatest that love can give; for greater love hath no man than this, that a man lay down his life for his friends.

3

All this is more fully exposed for us in the Epistle to the Hebrews, that great book which gives more explicit expression to the themes of priesthood and sacrifice that underlie the gospel record.

The central argument of the epistle is that in Christ we see the reality of priesthood and sacrifice, a reality contrasted with the shadows of the Aaronic priesthood of the old covenant. The mysterious figure of Melchisedek, the priest-king who suddenly appears in the Abraham saga, had suggested some better thing to come, though Melchisedek too only prefigures the real thing. In Christ alone is there true and effective priesthood.

Two things stand out. First, the essential nature of Christ's priesthood is to be seen in the fact that Christ offered *himself* in perfect obedience to his Father.[1] It is a personal dedication to the will of God the Father, a dedication as complete as possible, which is the offering desired by God from man, the worshipper: an offering perfectly made by the representative Man, the "New Adam" or "Son of Man" of the New Testament writers. He who offers that is the true priest, in whose self-oblation all sacrificial worship is purged of its dross and impurity. Secondly, Christ's is an *eternal* priesthood. He is declared to be a priest "for ever". His priestly work does not cease to be effective, when the act that gives it form and expression, the supreme act of Calvary, is performed and the historical event is over. That action does not need to be done again and again, as the ever-changing stream of time flows on, for it has an abiding dynamic effect. It is wholly sufficient to fulfil a universal, world-embracing purpose of redemption. No repetition of it is necessary, since it avails for all men. All can "enter into the holy place by the blood of Jesus, by the way which he dedicated for us, a new and living way".[2] "He, because he abideth for ever, hath his priesthood unchangeable. Wherefore also he is able to save to the uttermost them that draw near unto God through him, seeing he ever liveth to make intercession for them."[3]

The Epistle to the Hebrews, therefore, does not allow us to stop with the death on the cross in our understanding of

[1] See especially Heb. 10 and the use there made of Ps. 40.
[2] Heb. 10. 19, 20.   [3] Heb. 7. 24, 25.

our Lord's priesthood and sacrifice. We are to relate Calvary to the mystery of Christ exalted "at the right hand of the majesty on high". From early days this was clearly realized, as is best seen from the patristic ideas of the Eucharist and from the liturgies. It was a general view in the early Fathers that the sacrificial worship of the Eucharist really takes place in heaven, at the heavenly altar. The altars round which the Christians gather on earth are, as it were, a reflection, or projection into time and space, of the eternal centre of worship, the worship of heaven in which, with angels and archangels, redeemed humanity is gathered round its head, the glorified Son of Man, whose priesthood abides for ever. If, as has been persuasively argued,[1] the *Sanctus* was originally the climax of the eucharistic prayer, coming at the end, not at the beginning of the Canon, the primitive form of the Liturgy shows even more clearly than has been realized hitherto that it is in line with the Epistle to the Hebrews and, we may add, with the visionary splendours of the fourth chapter of the Apocalypse. In any event, the *Sursum Corda* is sufficient evidence of the primitive understanding of eucharistic worship.

So the Fathers lead us to think of the priesthood of Christ, and of his sacrifice, as regulative principles for the interpretation not only of Calvary but also of the work of the risen Christ. The horizon widens to include the resurrection, the ascension and heavenly session, the Eucharist. Christ, the eternal priest, is the consecrator at every Eucharist that has been or ever will be offered. Every Eucharist is, in a real sense, included in the one oblation of himself once offered. The inclusion is not, and cannot be, by way of repetition of that oblation. Rather we must say that the saving act of

[1] By Professor E. C. Ratcliff, *Journal of Ecclesiastical History*, vol. i, Nos. 1 and 2, 1950.

Calvary, which can never be repeated, is given effectual signification and personal application by the Lord himself, when in the earthly eucharistic rite the Christians show forth the Lord's death. For he, the living Christ, is a priest for ever, "after the order of Melchisedek".

4

There is a yet higher level to which Christian reflection upon the priesthood of Christ must endeavour to rise. That priesthood is linked with our most exalted thoughts about the crowning revelation, the mystery of the Holy and Undivided Trinity, which it serves to illuminate in a remarkable way.

The Christian revelation enables Christian faith to see within the eternal rhythm of the divine life the response of the Eternal Son to the Eternal Father as a response of perfect love and perfect joy. This response, as an eternal fact, is not to be described as "sacrificial", for sacrifice carries with it the idea of loss and belongs to the temporal order. Now in the sacrifice of Calvary the incarnate Son "loses" his life. When, that is to say, in the Incarnation, manhood is taken up into the Godhead for the redemption of the world, the response of the Son takes on the quality of sacrifice. So it must be in a sinful world, a world that needs redemption. Whatever formulation we give to the atoning work of Christ "for us men and for our salvation" we cannot escape the fact that it was done by a total self-offering involving a death as well as a life. Hence it is that sacrifice, a self-giving that renounces or surrenders all to God, becomes the mode of response proper to the *incarnate* life of the Eternal Son. And with sacrifice is involved mediation "for us men", and with mediation, priesthood, since a priest is one who speaks to God for man and to man for God.

Part of the meaning of that "self-emptying" of which St Paul writes [1] is to be seen here. The unchanging energy of love which is the life of the triune God appears in the incarnate life of the Son as self-sacrifice, humiliation, and vicarious suffering when the Son takes our nature upon him, being made like unto us in all things except sin. In this gracious self-emptying the unimaginable glory of the divine nature is made known to us, in terms of our own human condition; made known, that is, as infinite compassion, selfless love, and a generosity, of which the cross is the only measure. In the illumination of this sacrificial love we can know God as he is; not indeed with divine knowledge, but with a human knowledge that is sufficient to bring us to the creaturely response that is appropriate to our nature, the response of adoration and faith.

In that response our human nature is to find its true meaning and its proper consummation and fulfilment. As the earthly life of the Son of Man moves into the passion and the death, we are seeing the perfect manifestation of filial obedience. We are seeing that true humanity is a voluntary and loving doing "not of mine own will but of the will of him that sent me". And if we ask how that can be made to appear in us, being what we are, frail and sinful, how it can be an example for us to follow, how men can possibly be like the Son of God, the answer is that Christ comes to do *in* us what he does *for* us. He comes to give us a share in that new humanity through a new birth and a supernatural nurture. So he shares his Sonship with us and we become, as St Paul says, "adopted" sons.

So, too, he shares his priesthood and man can again fulfil his proper rôle of mediation. For man, by the pattern of his being, made "of the dust of the earth" and "in the image of

[1] Phil. 2. 7.

God" is essentially an intermediary. Rooted in the material order by his physical being, but transcending it by his intellectual and spiritual powers, he stands in the hierarchy of being as a connecting link between the temporal and the eternal. The great High Priest restores to us our priestly mediation, as spokesmen of nature and worshippers of God from within the order of nature. For the "first Adam" failed. He would not accept the conditions of his stewardship but aspired to be his own master, though the world in which he was set was God's possession not man's. He forfeited his place in the "garden", his appointed place in the material creation, and went into exile. The "Second Adam" puts man back where God would have him be, making him once more nature's priest. Of this restoration and its meaning we shall have more to say in what follows.

2

THE EXTENSION OF PRIESTHOOD

1

Christianity is an historical religion; it is rooted in the past, in a series of events that can be dated. But it does not stay there. The crucifixion is an historical occurrence, an incident that happened in the far-off days when Pontius Pilate was governor of Judea; but it is also a source of undying power, of spiritual radio-activity permeating all subsequent history. The works of Christ go on. That is the meaning of Pentecost, the Church, and the sacraments. They go on, not by discarding or supplanting the works of the incarnate life, but in applying their infinite content to the needs of successive generations. "The Spirit", says Christ, "shall take of mine, and shall declare it unto you." [1]

So it is that the priesthood of Christ, like his activity as teacher and prophet, is in perpetual operation in his Body, the universal Church. The one priest, the one mediator is a living, contemporary Christ. In what way, or ways, then, does he act, making his priesthood operative? That is the next stage in our inquiry.

Two closely connected, but distinguishable, lines of operation reveal themselves. They both proceed from the words and acts of Jesus in his earthly life.

The first belongs to the Church as a whole. Since to be a

---

[1] John 16. 14.

Christian is to be made a member of Christ and of his mystical Body, so that in the bold language of St Augustine the whole Christ is the head and the body, Christ and his Christians, the priesthood of Christ, like his sonship, is communicated to and exercised in the priestly community. So says the first Epistle of Peter, picking up the words of Exodus and claiming for the Church the priestly vocation of Israel, "ye are an elect race, a royal priesthood, a holy nation".[1] Hence there is what we may call a *baptismal priesthood*, common to the Church as a whole, distinguishable from the *ministerial priesthood* of the ordained bishop and presbyter because shared by every baptized man, woman, and child. All truly Christian activity, of hand or brain, social, political, economic, personal, is a work of priestly mediation in the name of Christ. For in its own measure and degree it should be done for the glory of God, on behalf of men, and for the welfare of mankind, in the name of God.

We shall be considering this more at length in later chapters. Meanwhile we must turn to that other mode in which the priesthood of Christ operates, the mode of *ministerial priesthood*. For Christ, who made the New Israel to rise out of the Old, also appointed an apostolic ministry to proclaim the Gospel and to shepherd the flock. No one reading the gospels can fail to observe that the call and training of the twelve stand side by side with Christ's own proclamation of the kingdom of God and with the mighty works that accompanied the proclamation. It is to a share in both the words and the works that he appoints them when he sends them out in his name.[2] We must therefore consider, in this and the next two chapters, the ministerial priesthood of the apostolic ministry. What does it mean that the

[1] 1 Pet. 2. 9; Ex. 19. 5, 6.   [2] Mark 3. 14, 15.

Church of God has a "clergy" as well as "laity"? What place has the ministry of the Word and Sacraments in the organic structure of Christianity? Why, if *one* only is "priest", namely Christ, and *all* are "priestly", namely the Church, are *some* set apart as "priests"? These are some of the questions that we shall try to answer.

2

An Anglican may be allowed to set his mind to work on the meaning of ministerial priesthood with the aid of his own formularies. If, using this liberty, we turn to the Thirty-Nine Articles of Religion, a respectable historical document, if not to-day as highly esteemed as it once was, we find that Article 23 lays it down that the ministry of the Word and Sacraments is for those who are "lawfully called and sent". Lawful calling and sending are then restated as meaning a choice and calling "by men who have public authority given unto them in the congregation to call and send ministers".

We must admit that as a scientific definition of the Christian ministry this is both vague and insufficient. It is inadequate even as a loose general statement about the ministry, for it tells us nothing of what constitutes "public authority" in this field, a point obviously of central importance. However, the Article has to be seen in its historical and controversial context. It is concerned with an immediate sixteenth-century problem. Its authors wished to repudiate those who in that troublous time rejected official ministries and Church authority in the making of ministers. It is rebutting the view that the ministry is purely "prophetic" in character and emerges unpredictably, by direct interior inspiration. It is so intent upon this rebuttal, and upon the necessity of ecclesiastical authority, that it says nothing of the need of an "inward call", a requirement which at other times the Anglican Reformers, like the continental Reformers, were concerned to emphasize.[1] We have, then, to look elsewhere for a statement of the qualifications of those who have "public authority" to call and send ministers. We shall find it in the Preface to the Ordinal.

In this Preface we have what is still a short summary, but one that condenses a considerable body of doctrine in its weighty decisive phrases. This doctrine is nothing new. The Preface states the intention of the Church of England to stand in the old ways, to retain and perpetuate that historic ministry of bishops, priests, and deacons which, it says, the Church of God has had "from the Apostles' time", and which is to be "continued and reverently used and esteemed". No one is to be ordained until he has been "called, tried, examined and known to have such qualities as are requisite". After this testing, those who are approved are admitted to holy orders "by lawful Authority"; and this ordination is "by publick prayer, with imposition of hands". The ordaining "Authority" has already been indicated in the earlier reference to bishops[2]; but, as though to leave no possible doubt on the matter, we have the explicit statement that no one not episcopally ordained, either "according to the Form hereafter following" or by former episcopal consecration or ordination, is to be accounted a lawful bishop, priest, or deacon. Naturally enough, nothing is said in so short a Preface about the distinctive functions

[1] See, for example, the questions addressed by the bishop to the candidates in the ordination rites of the Anglican Ordinal.

[2] We are not now concerned with Archbishop Cranmer's personal views about the dependence of bishops on the "godly Prince".

proper to each of these three orders of ministers. These functions and the continuity of meaning assigned to the several orders are clear from the ordination rites themselves. The text of the rites, notwithstanding their variations from earlier ordination rites, makes it sufficiently clear that bishops alone consecrate bishops and ordain priests and deacons; that priests are ordained to the ministry of the Word and Sacraments but have no power of ordaining apart from the bishop; that deacons are assistants to priests but, like their predecessors throughout Christian history, have no power to exercise what historically has been the central function of the priest, the consecration of the bread and wine in the Eucharist.

The principle underlying all this is unmistakable. It is the principle of successive commission, which has controlled the evolution of the Christian ministry wherever the hierarchical structure of bishops, priests, and deacons has been found. Indeed, though in variously modified forms, the principle has been observed even where that structure has been abandoned. There are Protestant Communions, lacking the threefold ministry, where the commissioning of new ministers is normally restricted to existing ministers.

It is a commonplace that, when we investigate origins, historical problems cluster round the phrase "from the Apostles' time", and that conclusive evidence for the direct creation of the threefold ministry by the original apostles is not forthcoming. Yet the clouds of dust raised by the controversial literature on this subject should not be allowed to obscure the historical probability of substantial truth underlying the loose phrase "from the Apostles' time".

That probability may be seen from the general lines of the Church's development in the early days. From at least the middle of the second century of our era the Church laid great stress upon what it called the "apostolic tradition". Behind its still growing "New Testament", behind its preaching and teaching, behind its central eucharistic worship, and also behind the ministry of bishops, presbyters, and deacons, there was this apostolic tradition, the source and ground of its faith, and also of its institutional structure and its liturgical worship. All was a *tradition*, a thing handed over; and this conception was applied to the Church's ministry as it was to the faith that the ministers preached and the worship over which they presided. Early in the second century St Ignatius the martyr speaks of the bishop "sitting in the place [or, with a variant reading, as a type] of God and the presbyters in the place of the council of the apostles", just as he urges his readers to be "grounded steadfastly in the decrees of the Lord and the apostles".[1] To know the truth of the Christian Gospel was to know the "apostolic" gospel, that faith which was steadfastly held in the "apostolic" churches and safeguarded by the "apostolic" ministry.

It would doubtless solve many problems if we could trace every step in the development from the ministry of the first generation of Christians to the hierarchy of the second century. But despite the blanks in our knowledge there is no evidence that the principle of commission, the handing on of authority to exercise ecclesiastical ministry by those already authorized, was at any time renounced; and such evidence as we have supports the hypothesis that the principle was taken for granted. For everywhere by the end of the second century the Church believed that functions assigned by the Lord to the apostles—pastoral oversight, authoritative teaching, and the commissioning of ministers —had been inherited by the local bishops.

[1] Ignatius, Ep. ad Magn. vi. 1. and xiii. 1.

We can, then, find a permanent core of truth in the statement that the Christian ministry goes back to "the Apostles' time". We are not going against the evidence if we regard it as an extension of the original apostolic ministry, established by the Lord, through the commissioning of new ministers at the hands of those who were themselves duly appointed ministers. This commissioning was in fact done, at least from the middle of the second century, if not exclusively yet normally, by episcopal consecration and ordination.[1] To be a minister meant to be incorporated into the apostolic ministry by episcopal ordination, before ever there was what we know as the New Testament, before ever the Nicene creed was compiled. In a wider sense there are, of course, other "ministries"; indeed, all Christians, are "ministers". But not all Christians participate in this apostolic ministry; that is true only of those who have received it "by publick prayer with the imposition of hands".

3

Why, then, does the Church no longer call her ministers "apostles"? Since she does not, what is the meaning of the term "apostolic" as applied to the threefold ministry of the Christian Church? In what sense does apostleship persist in the Church after the decease of the original group of persons to whom the New Testament gives the name of apostles? There are those who tell us that apostleship ceased to be after the first Christian generation. Is that the reason why thereafter we speak not of the apostles but of bishops, presbyters, and deacons?

[1] There is still dispute among ecclesiastical historians about, for example, certain Egyptian procedures and the meaning of the texts that describe them.

The evidence of the gospels makes it plain that the Lord committed to his twelve the proclamation of the Gospel and the care of the flock. The apostolate is an essential New Testament datum, as it is an essential element in the tradition called "apostolic" by the early Church. Nor is there any resisting the cumulative weight of the many New Testament passages that refer to the exalted status and authority of apostleship. Professor Karl Barth does not go too far when he says, "there is *one* fundamental ecclesiastical principle which cannot be denied without at the same time denying the resurrection of Christ and, in so doing, the very heart of the New Testament: the authority of the apostolate".[1] The apostles are appointed to be fishers of men, to be the stewards of the Lord's household, princes enthroned in the Messiah's kingdom, shepherds of the flock. St Paul has no hesitation in acting upon this majestic authority, as his correspondence with Corinth shows in the plainest terms.[2] The practical exercise of apostleship in the first Christian generation, illustrated in abundant detail in the epistles and in the Acts, is beyond the possibility of denial.[3]

But who are "apostles"? The mention of St Paul, not one of the Lord's twelve, is alone sufficient to raise the question. It does more. It indicates that we are not confined to the original (or the reconstituted) twelve; that the idea of apostleship grew and developed and that the evolution of the apostolate began in the first generation of Christians.

First and foremost, the early Church knew as apostles the group of twelve disciples appointed by the Lord Jesus

---

[1] *Church and State*, p. 57 (quoted by A. G. Hebert, *Form of the Church*, p. 109).

[2] Mark 1. 17, Luke 12. 42 (Matt. 24. 45), Luke 12. 29, 30, John 21. 15-7; 1 Cor. 4. 21, 5. 5, 2 Cor. 5. 20, 10. 8, 13. 2.

[3] The authority of the apostles is dealt with more fully in Part II, pp. 95-8.

himself in his earthly life and reconstituted by the choice of
St Matthias after the resurrection and ascension. The significance of the number is apparent. Here are the patriarchal
leaders and progenitors of the New Israel: here is the
renewal of the patriarchate side by side with the renewal of
the Covenant and the renewal of Israel, prefigured in the
sacred Torah.[1] But apostleship is also a wider term.

Direct commission from God adds to the eleven St
Matthias, appointed as he was by the sacred lot. Direct
commission also makes St Paul an apostle, as he vehemently
insists when his authority is questioned.[2] This first extension
of apostleship takes us beyond the earthly life of Jesus, as
does also the appointment of St James, the Lord's brother,
who is counted an apostle presumably because of his kins-
ship with the Lord (whatever the exact degree of kinship
may have been) and the special vision of the risen Christ
vouchsafed to him.[3]

Here, in these earliest holders of the office, we find
apostleship in its primary and most august form. But the
idea opens out further. The New Testament tells us of a
kind of junior apostleship, as we may call it; this appears in
St Barnabas, who with St Paul shares the apostolate of the
Gentiles.[4] Apostolic delegates of various kinds are often
referred to in the epistles of St Paul, in the Acts and in the
Pastoral Epistles.

Other ministries, of course, existed in the Church of the
first generation. It was only to be expected that many forms
of ministerial service and activity should spring spon-
taneously out of the life of the Church, without any specific
dependence on a direct command or appointment by the
Lord in his days on earth. We find in the New Testament

---

[1] Num. 1. 4–17, 7. 12–84, 10. 17–27, 17. 2–11.   [2] Gal. 1. 1.
[3] 1 Cor. 15. 7.   [4] Acts 14. 14.

that this did indeed happen. St Paul gives us more than once lists of such ministries. But there is no kind of hint that these forms of ministry took the place of the apostolate or acted independently of it. It would, in truth, be most strange and inexplicable that the Lord's own provision of apostles should be set aside and supplanted by these other ministries, either in the first or in later generations. In fact, we know enough of the first generation to make it certain that the apostles—first the twelve, then St Matthias, St Paul, St James, and their delegates—remained in the first place of authority.

When that first generation passed away, it is clear that in some of its original qualities apostleship could not be continued. The close connection of the first apostles with the Lord, by direct appointment in his earthly life, or before Pentecost, or in a special revelation, is their incommunicable privilege. So, too, is their personal testimony, as eyewitnesses, to the fact of the Lord's resurrection from the dead. But the New Testament plainly declares that the apostle has other essential functions, which can, and indeed must, be passed on. The continuation and extension of the Lord's work by commission from him is one such function.[1] Another is the proclamation of the Gospel to all nations.[2] A third is the pastoral oversight of the flock.[3] These are, in their own nature, transmissible elements in apostleship, no less plainly evidenced than the non-transmissible elements. They are not for the first Christian generation only. They are necessary in every generation. If the Church abides, they abide.

There is a deep significance in the fact that the Lord chose men to carry on his work. He wrote no book. He did not himself remain on earth, but ascended into heaven,

[1] Matt. 10.   [2] Matt. 28. 19.   [3] Luke 22. 25–30; John. 21. 15–17.

3

saying that it was expedient for the disciples that he should go away. In leaving men, he left the apostolate to his Church. He created the apostolate in and for his New Israel. If his work is to be done by those who speak in the name of the Lord and his chosen men, not merely in the name of any contemporary Christian group, the Church needs an *apostolic* ministry. It needs, that is to say, a ministry which receives the Lord's own authority at the hands of those who themselves have received it: Call and appointment are necessary, because that is how the Lord did it. There is only one apostle, in the originative sense, as there is only one priest, pastor, and teacher: Christ himself. But Christ continues his apostolic, priestly, pastoral, and teaching work through men. If the gospels are to be trusted, he did it, even while he was himself on earth; and he did it by the method of delegation and commission. Is it to be expected that this constructive method of his, so central in his recorded mission, was to be abandoned after the first generation?[1]

The gaps in the early evidence will always leave openings for denials of apostolic succession, both as fact and as principle. Those who accept it will do so because they cannot read the New Testament without being led to expect the development, under the guidance of the Holy Spirit, of a settled and permanent ministry proceeding from and continuous with the apostolate; and this, in fact, is what the early Church believed to have happened. They will accept, as from the Lord, a ministry established by Christ himself in and for his Church; a ministry which is an expansion and perpetuation of what he himself deliberately gave to us; a ministry that follows his own method of commission and

[1] A recent treatment of the succession by an English patristic scholar is Professor H. E. W. Turner's judicious discussion in his Bampton Lectures for 1954, *The Pattern of Christian Truth*, Lecture VI, esp. pp. 347f.

delegation of authority; a ministry that links us in the twentieth century with the words and works of Jesus, the one apostle of the Father, in his earthly ministry.

4

That is no small thing, no dispensable heritage. But there is another equally important principle, which must be held together with this principle of commission from ordainer to ordained, if the true nature of apostolic succession is to be seen.

There is no more essential principle for Christian thought than the truth that Christ remains for ever the living head of his Church. He alone is the one pastor and bishop and apostle in the full sense of these terms. Therefore what is done sacramentally, through human hands, in the ordination of ministers is always his action, a renewal or delegation by him of his own apostolate. Apostolic succession, it must be emphasized, is not adequately expressed in terms of a chain. The image is doubly insufficient. It is defective, because it suggests an ever-increasing distance from Christ as well as connection with Christ. Again, it has the obvious weakness of any merely mechanical metaphor, namely, that any one missing or imperfect link breaks the chain. If that were all that catholic Christians meant by apostolic succession, it would be an untenable belief; for we could never guarantee historically that the chain was one hundred per cent reliable, that it had never been broken by the negligence or the dishonesty of even one ordaining bishop.

Succession from ordainer to ordained is only one aspect of the matter. The ordainer is always Christ himself, validating the sacramental acts of his apostolic representatives within his Body the Church. The horizontal line of temporal succession meets the vertical line of divine action when in the praying congregation the bishop lays his hands upon those who are being admitted to holy orders. Christ is no dead hero of the past, but the living Lord of his sacramental Church.

The Church militant lives in time and the generations come and go. So succession, tradition, communication—the modes proper to spatio-temporal existence—are the inevitable modes of our participation in the historical revelation and in the life of the redeemed community. But the living Christ, the same yesterday, to-day, and to-morrow, still gives the apostolate to his people. It is not an apostolate utterly disconnected with that of Peter and James and John but the same apostolate; and it is a very precious thing, this perpetuation of what Jesus initiated in Galilee, in ever-expanding impact on successive generations of Christian people. But it is always Christ's apostolate, the apostolate that by nature belongs solely to him who was born of the Virgin Mary, suffered under Pontius Pilate, rose again from the dead, and now lives and reigns with the Father in the unity of the Holy Spirit.

3

THE APOSTOLIC MINISTRY AND PRIESTHOOD

We have seen that the foundation of Christian priesthood is laid in the one originative priesthood of Jesus Christ. Its application to the needs of the Church in each generation of Christians is made through the apostolic ministry which Christ has given to his Church; a ministry which is the extension or expansion of the apostolate established by him in the days of his flesh. And we have seen that this extension is by the gracious acts of the Lord himself, the ordainer of all ministers, in a sacramental mode whereby those who themselves hold his commission pass it on to others. By common consent, from the second century to the sixteenth, the bishops of the Church were accounted the holders of the apostolic office, in so far as that office was an abiding structural element in the Church; and they ordained presbyters and deacons for a delegated ministry, each order at its own level, reserving for the episcopate the continuation of apostolic ministry by the laying-on of the bishop's hands with public prayer.

The original functions of these three orders of ministers have some marked differences from those which they fulfil in modern times. The primitive bishop was normally the regular pastor and liturgical minister of the local Christian congregation.

It was he who presided at the Sunday Eucharist, preached the liturgical sermon, taught and baptized catechumens, and in fact did most of what the modern parish priest regards as his ordinary work. The presbyter was still a member of a group or college, and each bishop had his "senate" of presbyters. They assisted him in his pastoral and liturgical functions. It was they rather than the bishop himself who carried on—though, naturally, on a much smaller scale than in later ages—that organizing and administrative business which to-day we regard as the heaviest burden of the episcopate. The deacons were the immediate attendants on the bishop; the office of archdeacon still survives as a witness to that relationship, though archdeacons have for centuries been normally in priest's orders. Deacons were not "assistant curates", each under the direction of a single presbyter-incumbent, and they did not all expect to be ordained priest after a year in the diaconate.

We cannot here trace the historical developments whereby the presbyter became the normal priest and pastor of the local congregation and the diaconate became simply a preparation for the presbyterate, as a result of the political and social changes that caused the bishops to withdraw from the local pastorate and to become the administrative heads of large districts. Enough to say that the changes were the direct result of the growth of the Church and of its recognition by the Roman Empire. They did not affect the essence of the threefold ministry. The bishop still retained his specific functions of ordination and confirmation. The presbyter was still the pastoral and liturgical collaborator of the bishop. The deacon still remained the assistant of the other ministers.

Bishops and presbyters, then, have always been associated in a common ministry to the Christian people, though with certain significant reservations to the episcopate. If we concentrate attention upon the common elements, pastoral, liturgical, evangelistic, and so on, in the ministry exercised by bishops and presbyters, how are we to characterize that ministry? In particular, are we to say that it is essentially "priestly" or "sacerdotal" or that it is not? I have referred many times to "priesthood", but I have not yet given any definitive account of what priesthood is. It is high time that we turned to that part of our study.

From the second century onwards it became the normal practice to use the ordinary word for priest (*hiereus* in Greek, *sacerdos* in Latin) primarily for the Christian bishop, but also, somewhat later, for the Christian "elder" or presbyter. The superior status of the bishop was commonly indicated by calling him the high priest. Generally speaking, from the time of the third- and fourth-century Fathers the bishop and the presbyter were universally regarded as having a sacerdotal character.

Why did this happen? Was it a departure from the original Christian idea of the ministry? Was it caused by a dubious analogy with the Jewish priesthood of the old covenant? Or was it a recognition of the fact that priesthood is inherent in the Christian ministry?

There was certainly, from a very early date, an interest in noting the parallel between the Jewish high priest, priests, and levites and the Christian bishop, presbyters, and deacons. But this analogy was not what justified the priestly interpretation of the Christian ministry. The ground of that interpretation lies in the Gospel and in the relation of the ministry to Christ.

What is priesthood? Empirically speaking, from the standpoint of the comparative study of religion, we find that in the complex of ideas and practices and institutions commonly called religious there constantly appears the figure of the priest. He is a person who on the one hand is closely concerned with *cultus*, the rites and ceremonies of religious worship, and on the other hand with the knowledge of sacred things. In both respects he acts as a go-between or mediator, speaking to God for man and to man for God. In so describing the priest, we raise three fundamental questions of religion.

First, the priest is concerned with cultus. But how ought man to worship God? Secondly, the priest is concerned with the knowledge of sacred things. But what is the truth about God? Thirdly, the priest is a mediator. But how does man come to God?

According to Christianity, Jesus Christ provides, and in his own person fully and finally embodies, the true answer to all these questions. He, as man, gives, and enables his followers to give, true and acceptable worship to his Father. He teaches, and he is, himself, the truth of God. He is also the one mediator between God and man. In all these respects he fulfils, wholly and completely, the idea or image of priesthood. Priesthood is truly realized only in him and the priesthood not only of paganism but also of Israel is but a shadow of that reality which is the priesthood of Christ.

This is the teaching of the Epistle to the Hebrews. But it is also Christ's own teaching about himself, teaching given with peculiar force and solemnity as his earthly ministry drew to its climax. This is apparent if we consider the meaning of Christ's actions and words at the Last Supper.

The context is the Passover, a context of sacrifice.[1] The Lord's death is imminent. At the Last Supper, over the bread and the cup, he speaks the words that St Paul and

---

[1] This is true whether or not we identify the Last Supper with the Passover meal.

St Mark have recorded for us. They must have seemed very strange words to those who heard them, but their implication was soon to become clear. The seventeenth chapter of St John's Gospel is evidence enough. Jesus was telling his disciples that his death was not to be regarded as a disastrous calamity, the final proof of the failure of his mission; on the contrary they were to see in it a redemptive sacrifice, the Covenant-sacrifice sealing the new Exodus from the bondage not of an Egyptian Pharaoh but of the direst enemies of mankind, sin and death. Jesus in fact declares himself to be the messianic priest-leader, self-consecrated as victim, so that he is at once priest and sacrifice. Priesthood and sacrifice thus supply the images indicated by Christ himself as apt to describe his saving work. He is the mediator. He is the priest. He is the sacrifice. And the Christians are to be made one with him in his sacrifice, as they receive his sacrificial life as their sustenance and eat his Body and drink his Blood. The imagery is derived from the ancient Law. Where else could it come from, if Christ was to be the fulfilment of the promises of God to Israel? It had to be that "beginning from Moses and from all the prophets, he interpreted to them in all the Scriptures the things concerning himself".[1]

All this is decisive not only for Christology and for the doctrine of the Atonement but also for our understanding of the Church and the Ministry. The Church is the Body of Christ and the Fellowship of the Holy Ghost, as St Paul teaches. As such, it exists to unite itself with Christ in his obedience to the Father, his self-oblation. Focally it does this in its eucharistic worship, but also, through the inspiration and control of the Eucharist, it offers itself in its daily life, in the manifold activities of its several members. It thus

[1] Luke 24. 27.

shares corporately in the priesthood and victimhood of Christ, presenting itself as a living sacrifice, which is its "reasonable service" or "spiritual worship".[1] The primary function of the Church is this worship of God, as Christ teaches.[2] In Christ, redeemed humanity resumes the office from which Adam fell, the office of the priest of nature, the mediator between God and his material creation. For man is by design such a mediator, and in the new humanity which is Christ's and which is ours also "by adoption" we see the royal priesthood of the children of God.

So, too, when we come to think about the Christian ministry we cannot escape from priesthood, simply because it is a ministry of Christ the priest. The apostolic messengers and ministers of Christ represent and serve the whole Christ. There is neither more nor less reason for calling a duly authorized Christian minister a pastor or a preacher than for calling him a priest. He is all three, because he speaks in Christ's name, by his authority, in his apostolic service. Let it be repeated with all possible emphasis that this ministry is only that of a representative and a delegate, that no human priest can speak or act in his own name. Nor can any human preacher or pastor speak or act in his own name. In the full and originative sense there is only one pastor, the Good Shepherd; only one rabbi, preacher, leader, the Man of Nazareth; so too there is only one priest, that one true Israelite who gave his life a ransom for many, he who is at once Son of God, Lamb of God, and Son of Man.[3] But the apostolic commission is a sharing and a delegation of derived pastorate, evangelism, and priestly mediation, since Christ is one and indivisible. If we are thinking of bishop or presbyter as servants of Christ, we may properly call them ministers. If we think of their function

[1] Rom. 12. 1.   [2] Matt. 4. 10, 22, 37.   [3] Matt. 23. 8–10.

as undershepherds, they are pastors. If we think of them as proclaiming the Gospel, they are preachers of the Word. But they are priests too, because they speak and act for Christ, the great High Priest, the mediator, both in the eucharistic oblation and in the whole ministerial life. On the whole, we may claim that "priest" is the most biblical and the most evangelical of all these titles of the Christian bishop or presbyter; for it brings us closest to the saving work of God in Christ, to the cross and the atonement, and so to the very heart of the Gospel.

Only if we arbitrarily insist on interpreting priesthood in terms of savage rites, the slaughter of animals, a monopoly of divine truth, ecclesiastical tyranny, and so on, shall we deny that priesthood is a valid category for the under-standing of the Christian ministry. Yet so to interpret it is, from the New Testament and Christian point of view, mere topsy-turvydom, a transposition of shadow and substance. Priesthood is truly known by looking at Christ, at what he is and does, not at the levitical or any non-Christian priest.

With priesthood goes sacrifice. If the Christian ministry is priestly, it is also sacrificial. What are we to understand by this ancient and universal institution of religion and what has it to do with Christianity?

St Thomas Aquinas, following St Augustine, says that sacrifices are properly called when anything is done about things offered to God.[1] That is a very wide general defini-tion, intended to cover the multitudinous variations of the sacrificial element in religion. Within the Jewish religion itself, as every reader of the Bible knows, there was an elaborate system of sacrifices and the New Testament draws freely from this system in the imagery it applies to Christ. He is the Passover lamb, the sin-offering of the Day

[1] S.T. ii–ii. 85. 1 and 3.

of Atonement, the scapegoat, the Lamb of God.[1] Nothing
indeed more clearly illustrates the truth that the New
Testament derives pictorial imagery from the Old Testament to such an extent that without the Old Testament
it is unintelligible. But can we give more precision to St
Thomas' very general statement? We can if we take the
word "sacrifice" to pieces and observe that it derives from
two Latin words which mean "to make holy" (*sacrum facere*).[2]
How is something "made holy"? The underlying notion
seems to be by handing it over to God. A French theologian
has described the essence of sacrifice as a religious transfer
of property.[3] Man, that is to say, hands over to God some
precious possession which, because it is valued, is in some
sense part of himself and can represent him. By this renunciation man transfers the thing altogether into God's
possession so that, in one way or another, out of this tran-
saction divine blessing may be obtained and communion
with God established or restored. In some kinds of sacrifice
the thing given is in part returned to man as the means or
pledge of divine favour; and if the thing given is some kind
of food, it may in this kind of sacrifice become the material
of a sacred meal. Renunciation, cost, and loss, however, are
always involved in sacrifice. In *animal* sacrifice—and it
needs hardly be said that by no means all religious sacrifices
have been made by the offering of animals—the killing of
the animal was a preliminary to the sacrificial act proper,
because it was the way in which the transference of property
seemed possible. The life of the animal, which was identified

[1] 1 Cor. 5. 1, 1 Pet. 1. 18, John 18 and 19; Mark 14. 24, 1 Pet. 1. 2, Heb.
9. 19–20; Rom. 3. 21–6, Heb. 9. 26, 10. 11; 1 Pet. 2. 24, cf. 2 Cor. 5. 21;
John 1. 27.
[2] Etymologically, *sacrum facere* need not mean more than "to do the
sacred thing". But the meaning "to make holy" is not widely different,
since the doing of the sacred thing is an action involving the offering of
something to God.
[3] E. Masure, *Le Sacrifice du Chef* (Eng. trans., *The Christian Sacrifice*).

with the blood, had to be allowed to escape to God. Furthermore, the killing of the animal did decisively bring about the loss of property, without which the transference from one owner to another could not be made. But blood-shedding and death are not invariable and necessary parts of sacrifice as such.

We need not attempt to determine here and now whether this interpretation of sacrifice covers all and every kind of sacrificial action in the history of religion. It clearly explains a great deal of what men have felt and done in their approach to the divine. It enables us to gain a more sympathetic understanding of what at first sight seems to modern man, where animal sacrifice is concerned, a repellent and distasteful affair, mere butcher's business intruding into the worship of God. Its principal merit, however, is that it serves as a pointer to certain fundamental religious needs and to certain abiding values in the welter of sacrificial rites and customs.

We have already suggested that the prophetic movement in ancient Israel came to a certain dissatisfaction with the sacrificial system. What the system aimed at was right and true—man's service of God in loving obedience, man's use of his possessions not merely for his own satisfaction but as means to the worshipful doing of the divine will. But its method was defective, because it stopped short of that total dedication of the self in life and thought which is the only proper response of the creature to his Creator. It put in place of that a limited surrender of possessions. Suppose, now, that this total dedication of self could be realized. Then what the sacrifices of the Law blunderingly and partially sought to do would be achieved. It was achieved by one man, the Second Adam, the incarnate Son of God.

Here again, as with its correlative, priesthood, so with sacrifice. It comes to its true and full meaning only in

Christ. He, by the perfect offering of himself to his Father in life and in death, perfectly fulfils the meaning of sacrifice. Sacrifice truly understood is self-sacrifice, the offering of the will, the love that holds back nothing and, since the world is sinful, suffers all that must be suffered. This is the sacrifice that lies at the heart of the Christian Gospel and finds its climax on the cross. And this is the sacrifice that finds its effectual signification in the Eucharist. There is no new sacrifice, additional to the sacrifice on the cross, when a Christian priest stands at the altar to offer the Christian sacrifice. Only the ritual presentation is renewed there day by day. But in that ritual presentation Christ the sacrifice is present in his sacramental Body and Blood. The cross masters the Eucharist, swings it into the orbit of its sacrificial dynamism, when the bread and wine become sacramentally the very Body and Blood. What Christ offered, on Calvary, we offer in the Eucharist: Christ himself and, because of our redemption, ourselves in and with him. And the human priest who is the spokesman and representative in the offering has sacrifice in all its Christ-given fullness to "show forth" as the ritual action of the Eucharist proceeds from the offertory through the thanksgiving and the breaking of the bread to the communion.

Only one priest, only one sacrifice. But these things live and are given effectual signification in the mystical Body of Christ and through the apostolic ministry. If the *words*, priest and sacrifice, sound archaic to modern ears, no doubt we might find other words, though it must be remembered that these words come to us with all the authority of the biblical revelation. But we can never abandon the *things* for which these words stand. For the things are the very stuff of the saving Gospel, of which the central symbol is the cross of Jesus Christ, the great High Priest.

4

THE OFFICE AND WORK OF A PRIEST

Thus far we have been concerned with the biblical and theological foundations of that ministerial priesthood which Christ has set in his Church. Before we pass on to the other and no less important mode in which the priesthood of Christ manifests itself—in what I have called baptismal priesthood, the corporate priesthood of the mystical Body of Christ—there is something to be said about what it means, in life and work, to be a ministerial priest.

We defer to Part II, addressed primarily *ad clerum*, some more detailed consideration of that indispensable spiritual discipline by which the ministerial life is shaped and nourished.

If the clergyman is to some extent a man apart, it is not the result of any deliberate mystification. Anyone can discover what he is supposed to be and to do by looking at the rite for the ordination of priests in the Ordinal attached to the Book of Common Prayer. If we examine, in particular, the bishop's address to the candidates, we shall find that, despite the now archaic Tudor English, it contains a clear and firm presentation of the priestly office.

The high dignity, the weighty office and charge to which these men are called are summarized in the words messengers, watchmen, and stewards. These are all biblical similes, and they all express ways in which the priest, according to his office, speaks from God to man. The other, complementary side of his work, that of bringing men to God, is mentioned a little further on in the charge, though it is obviously implied in the priest's functions as leader in liturgical worship, as the reconciler of penitent sinners, and as the man of prayer, which of course includes the mediatorial work of intercession.

For God to man; for man to God. That is the general pattern of the priest's work. What does it involve, when we begin to fill in the outline?

We may begin our answer to that question by considering the priest in his liturgical work. The first way in which Christ acts through his human priests is in the Liturgy. It is in the Liturgy, with its centre in the Eucharist, that the Church exercises its highest privilege, the corporate worship of God by the redeemed community, the messianic people of the Lord. We shall have more to say on this subject and on the formative place of the Liturgy in the Christian life in the last chapter of Part I. Here we confine ourselves to the priest's part in this supreme activity of the Christian Church.

The primary task of the priest is to maintain and commend this worship of God, and in it to fulfil his own proper part, which has its climax in the consecration of the Eucharist. No doubt this truth can be exaggerated and distorted; by isolating this function we can represent the priest as a merely ceremonial functionary. The mass-priest of the medieval chantry-system came perilously near to this impoverishment of priesthood and made it necessary to recover the ancient emphasis (we find it in the Anglican Ordinal) on the pastoral side of priesthood.[1] Over-specialization brought about the virtual isolation of this one duty,

[1] The ancient emphasis is clearly seen in St John Chrysostom's treatise *On the Priesthood*.

the eucharistic sacrifice, from the total content of ministerial priesthood. The balance had to be redressed. Yet it is true that the eucharistic sacrifice is the heart of the priest's specific part in public worship. Not that he offers it alone, while the people just look on. That is no part of sound Catholic doctrine but a parody and a caricature. The Eucharist is the oblation of the Church, not only of the clergy. The priest, however, has the ineffable privilege of being the hands and the voice of Christ, the head of the Church. Whether it is theoretically possible that there should be a Eucharist without a priest, who shall say? Certainly God is not bound by his ordinances for man. What we may say, however, is that Christ has set priests in his Church to do this work in the congregation of his priestly people, and that it is here that we touch the very heart and centre of the priest's ministry.

Surrounding the Eucharist in the Church's liturgical life is that structure of supplementary prayers and meditations which we know as the divine office. In the English Church it has been reduced to two elements, Morning and Evening Prayer. This simple pattern is not entirely novel. It takes us back in liturgical history to fourth-century Jerusalem. However, the simplification newly contrived in the English Prayer Books of the sixteenth and seventeenth centuries was not merely a return to ancient precedents; it had the very laudable intention of making the divine office more practicable for the laity. It was a change made for good pastoral reasons, in order that the office might be restored to its proper place as part of the Church's daily prayer, instead of being almost entirely a clerical and monastic devotion. Yet here too there is a special responsibility for the priest. What can only be *commended* to the laity, whose days are full of other activities, is strictly *enjoined* upon all priests and deacons.[1] Here again we see the special function of the priest in the maintenance of that worship of God whereby the Church lives and knows itself to be what it is: the holy nation, the royal priesthood, and the family of God. As the priest faithfully and regularly recites the daily offices, whether or not he has the assistance of some of the faithful, he bears his unceasing testimony to the first and great commandment, to love God in loving voluntary attention to his will and submission to his grace.

Are we again running the risk of interpreting the priest-hood in terms of the sanctuary and the sacristy? Not if we get all this in due perspective. It is fitting and good that the setting of this priestly work of worship should be as rich and gracious as we can make it. This will account for the Church's use of noble buildings, beautiful vestments, dignified ceremonies, and so on. And all these things will call for time and trouble on the priest's part if they are to be reverently handled, without casual negligence and sloven-liness. But all these things are secondary and unessential. A priest, be it said with all emphasis, is not a professional purveyor of religious pageants, complete with sermon and a collection. He is just as much a priest when he says Evensong in a train, returning from some meeting, as when he sings a solemn Eucharist in a cathedral or preaches a Lent course in Westminister Abbey.

We can turn next to the other side of the picture and consider the complementary relation between the priest and the people of God. As priest, he speaks for God to men, as well as for men to God. He has the exacting duty of preach-ing the Gospel. Others may indeed preach and perhaps preach better than the priest. But he preaches as part of his

---

[1] See the concluding regulations in the Preface to the B.C.P., "Con-cerning the Service of the Church".

proper ministry in the Church, bearing witness as best he can to the saving Gospel and the divine revelation, which he is commissioned by Christ in his Church to make known to all who will hear. Preaching is not the exploiting of oratorical gifts by professional spellbinders, gathering round them groups of admiring disciples. Nor is it simply instruction out of dogmatic textbooks or exhortations to good behaviour. The priest does not go into the pulpit to commend his own views on things in general. He will need to learn and practise the arts of the speaker, the teacher, and the counsellor. But primarily his preaching is a real mediatory office, a showing of Jesus Christ to men. He must always, even when he uses to the full all the personal gifts he may have, point men away from himself to the divine Lord of the Church. His art must be directed to this one objective, the turning of men's hearts and minds to Christ as the way, the truth, and the life.

The minister of the Word is also the minister of the Sacraments. In baptism and penance, he is the minister of Christ initiating newcomers into the life of the redeemed community and restoring to the fellowship those who have fallen away from it. He gives Christ's blessing to man and wife as they enter on holy matrimony. He brings Christ's strengthening and healing touch to the sick in holy unction. Most frequent and characteristic of all his sacramental ministries is the giving of Holy Communion, both normally in the course of the eucharistic rite and in the extension of communion by means of the reserved sacrament. In all this Christ is at work and the human priest is his ministerial representative. His personal gifts and graces, his elegant accomplishments and social charm may be great or small but all that has very little relevance to this fundamental part of his ministry. Reverence and humility, unfailing readiness to minister in courtesy and charity, self-forgetfulness in the exercise of so great a privilege—these are the things for which the priest prays as he goes about his business as minister of Christ's sacramental gifts.

Yet all this—and it is exacting enough—is not by any means the end of the story.

Beyond the altar and the font, the confessional and the sick communion, there is the endless diversity of the priest's ministry to his people, in groups and as individuals, in all the vicissitudes and crises of human life from childhood to the grave. Like the physician of the body, but in a field even more delicate and complicated than the doctor's, he has to be the teacher, counsellor, shepherd of all sorts and conditions of men. He is always liable to be called upon, and there is no forty-hour week for the physician of souls. He may be summoned to minister to a dying saint, close to God and spiritually far more advanced than himself, and pass on at once to teach a class of children or listen to some unhappy woman's sordid tale of domestic misery. The tax upon his resources, his patience, and his sympathy, his charity and knowledge, is heavy and it is endless. There are no simple answers, and no official forms to be passed over the counter in dealing with human souls. The *tempo* may be slower for the country priest than for the vicar of a big urban parish; but the country priest has few of the helpers that the town priest can usually find and he may have two or three parishes under his care, with long distances to cover in all weathers, so that his work is often just as arduous and his day just as full as his town colleague's.

It is in this kind of pastoral ministry that we get a glimpse of the inner reality of ministerial priesthood. It is comparatively easy to describe the outward activities of the clergy, bewildering though they are in their diversity and their number. But the priesthood has an inner side, more difficult to write about, yet vital for the understanding of what priesthood truly is.

To attempt a brief description, we may venture to say that priesthood is the imitation of Christ as priest and victim. The ministerial priest is not just a religious functionary, a professional who goes back into "private life" when he puts his stole back in the sacristy cupboard. He must live his priesthood. He must do and he must suffer, not to win any earthly reward or even what is called success in his ministry, but simply because he represents Jesus Christ, the priest and victim. Those priests in whom we see the examples of our human priesthood, a Benson or a Wainwright or a Curé d'Ars, are not successful officials of religious organizations but men who lived out, day by day, in the streets and houses of their parishes, the same holy dedication that they fulfilled each morning at the altar of their parish church. In the last resort it is sacrifice, self-oblation, holiness that the priest of Jesus Christ must see and desire as the quality of his priesthood. Doing is for him but the outward expression of being. Every priest who knows what his priesthood really means knows himself to be a failure and an unprofitable servant; and he knows at the same time that this is no excuse for giving up, but rather is a spur to that penitence which is the seed of fidelity. An ever greater fidelity to his dedication, not any visible success or personal aggrandizement, is the only way of being a minister of him who emptied himself that he might save the world.

Happy the parish whose priests so fulfil their office. And happy the priest whose people can and do enter, with sympathy and appreciation, into an understanding of what their ministers wish to do and to be.

5

THE PRIESTHOOD OF ALL BELIEVERS

In the first chapter we said that priesthood is an essential
category for the understanding of Jesus Christ and of the
Christian profession, no less than for the understanding of
the ordained ministry of the Church. We went on to consider the priesthood of the ordained ministry and now we
turn to what we called the baptismal priesthood, the priesthood of all believers.

The priesthood of all believers is a phrase that became a
slogan in the polemics of the protestant Reformation, but of
course the idea is no sixteenth-century novelty. It has the
most respectable ancestry in the Fathers of the Church and
in the New Testament. If any doctrine can be called
catholic, this is assuredly one of them, for it is integral to the
catholic doctrine of the Church as the mystical Body of
Christ.

1

We must look, first, at the foundations of this vital truth
in the Bible. We need not again dwell upon the fact that
the priesthood of the faithful, like the priesthood of the
apostolic ministry, can be spoken of only in subordination to
the priesthood of Christ, the one High Priest. As we have
tried to make plain throughout, there is no other priesthood,
in the full sense, but his. Christ's priesthood is communi-

cated to the whole body of his people in one mode, as it is to his apostolic ministers in another. In both cases the priesthood of men is derivative and dependent.

There is a parallel with the sonship of our Lord. He, the only Son, gives us a share in his sonship; and what is his by essential nature is ours only by grace and favour, as it is also limited by our creatureliness. St Paul's way of putting it is to say that we are sons "by adoption". Christ, who is of one substance with the Father, and co-equal with the Father, is the Son of God in a sense in which no created being can be Son of God. Yet as members of Christ we may share in his sonship to the full extent of our human and creaturely capacity.

In the Epistle to the Hebrews we find the sonship and the priesthood of our Lord brought into close association. In chapter 5 the author quotes two passages from the psalms, "Thou art my Son, this day have I begotten thee" (Ps. 2. 7) and "Thou art a priest forever after the order of Melchisedek" (Ps. 110. 4). Both these prophetic images are seen to be realized in Christ; and the writer then goes on to say that it is just the perfection of Christ's sonship, as manifested in the conditions of the incarnate life, that equipped Him—if we may use such a phrase—to be "named of God a high priest after the order of Melchisedek" (Heb. 6. 10). The Son of God, who is also the Son of Man, in the perfection of his Sonship, is thereby the perfect mediator, the perfect priest.

Since, then, sonship and priesthood are indissolubly united in Christ, the new man, we can say that the Church which is his Body partakes of both characters. By baptism we enter into our sonship "by adoption" and into our priestly status. Some of the Fathers of the Church, for example St Cyril of Jerusalem and St Augustine, liked to point out the deeper significance of our common label of "Christians". To be a Christian is not only to accept certain beliefs and practices or to be a member of a distinctive religious society: it is to share the priestly anointing of Jesus. For Christ means the Anointed One, and priests were anointed under the old Law. So Christians are those who are anointed with the same divine unction as made Jesus the Christ a priest. St Cyril says, in his treatise *On Worship in Spirit and in Truth*, that only the baptized may enter the inner sanctuary and offer to God spiritual sacrifices. He echoes there the teaching of Hebrews [1] which describes the priestly church, "having therefore, brethren, boldness to enter into the holy place by the blood of Jesus, by the way which he dedicated for us, a new and living way, through the veil, that is to say, his flesh; and having a great high priest over the house of God; let us draw near with a true heart in fulness of faith having our hearts sprinkled from an evil conscience, and our body washed with pure water".

If we now turn to the first Epistle of Peter we find the corporate priesthood of the Church enriched by a further idea, that of royalty. The Church is a royal priesthood, fulfilling the vocation of Israel to be "an elect race, a royal priesthood, a holy nation".[2] For Christ is anointed king as well as anointed priest and the Church has a derived and dependent viceroyalty. This ancient image of kingship indicates that the Church has to exercise leadership and representation in the world as well as mediation and ministry. For the king exists to lead his people into the common good of all. The entry of our High Priest into the heavenly sanctuary at his ascension is the taking possession of his heavenly kingdom; and he enables his followers to share his kingdom.

[1] Heb. 10. 19–22.   [2] 1 Pet. 2. 9; Ex. 19. 5.

So the lost royalty of the "first Adam" is restored to us in the "Second Adam". The imagery of the first two chapters of Genesis shows us, as we have suggested earlier in this book, the pattern and design of man. He is, in the intention of God, the priest of nature and the vicegerent of God in that part of the created universe to which he belongs. When he rebels against his subordination to his Maker and claims to be his own master, he produces only confusion. He is degraded from his priestly office and he also loses his royalty. He can no longer rule himself, but is ruled by his discordant passions. He misuses natural things and makes them the means of further degradation. He cannot mediate between God and his creatures as the wise steward of his Master's household. But in Christ the lost royalty is restored. He who enables men to offer themselves as a holy, living, acceptable sacrifice to God and so to give the spiritual worship for which they are made, also enables them to recover the true use and control of natural things, instead of being enslaved by them. And he makes the Church, which is his new creation, once again the mediator, bringing men to God and God to men, as it seeks to persuade all the sinful sons of Adam to accept the kingship of God and his Christ. For the Church is the nucleus of redeemed humanity, irradiating from the centre the light and life of Christ in whatever measure and degree men are willing to receive it. All Christian activity, in its deepest impact upon the life of men, should be the work of human liberation, extending the rule of God, which is perfect freedom, throughout the whole domain of man's spiritual and bodily life.

Here is the restoration of the divine image which has been defaced by man's claim to autonomy. Here is that imparted share in the royalty of his Creator which goes with man's stewardship over the earth. It is a conditional and limited control and it will never be complete or absolute. But it makes the Christians the salt and leaven of human society, wherever they bring their royal priesthood into effective action.

If we now go from the Epistle to the Hebrews and the first Epistle of Peter to the gospels, we find in the events that ushered in our Lord's earthly ministry the fountainhead of the royal priesthood of his Church. After his baptism by John, which the Church has seen as prefiguring Christian baptism, the Son of God is anointed by the Father himself with the divine unction of the Holy Spirit. This is comparable to the anointing of a priest, for it is preceded, like that of Aaron, by a ritual ablution and is introductory to the public ministry. So Jesus himself affirms in the synagogue at Nazareth, when he applies to himself the words of Isaiah 61: "The Spirit of the Lord is upon me, because he anointed me to preach good tidings to the poor; he hath sent me to proclaim release to the captives and recovering of sight to the blind, to set at liberty them that are bruised, to proclaim the acceptable year of the Lord." As the priests of the Old Israel "proclaimed Torah", so the Lord's Anointed proclaims the good tidings of God's redeeming work. It is also a royal anointing, for it inaugurates the preaching and the diffusion of a new kingdom, the kingdom of God and of Christ. Against the claims of the devil to command the kingdoms of this world Jesus, the true king of men, begins in the wilderness his victorious warfare of liberation. To his Church he commits that same warfare and that same priestly and royal anointing by the Spirit, with the promise "he that believeth on me, the works that I do shall he do also; and greater works shall he do, because I go to the Father".[1]

[1] John 14. 12.

2

With this analysis, brief and incomplete as it is, of the biblical material it is possible to shape some general conclusions about baptismal priesthood. In the next chapter, on the apostolate of the laity, we shall be concerned mainly with some practical applications. The rest of the present chapter will try to draw out a few of the guiding principles by which practical Christian action should be directed.

First then the priesthood of the Church means that the Church in its essential nature is to be the place of spiritual sacrifice. The general form of the Christian life is to be understood as a life of sacrificial charity. The *content* of sacrifice is ourselves in Christ. In Christ, for only in him, in penitent and faithful surrender to his renewing power, can we make any offering. He must unite us to himself and lead us to the Father. Then, and then only, can we offer that worship of which St Paul wrote to the Roman Christians, presenting our bodies a living sacrifice. The *sacrament*, that is, the expressive, dynamic, and effectual sign of sacrifice, is the Eucharist. There, in those holy mysteries, the Christians find themselves. They know what they are and for what they exist. In that sacrificial renewing by the Body and Blood of Christ they constantly revive the impulse and the power to return to their sacrificial living in the world. There is no Christianity without sacrifice; and sacrifice in this life carries with it suffering and loss, the cross-bearing which the disciples must undertake with their Master.

Cross-bearing is, from one point of view, a mortification, a death to sin. It brings with it the discipline of ourselves and the costly demands of self-sacrifice for others. Self-pleasing and self-seeking in all their forms are to be renounced. Our corrupt egocentricity is to give place to a thorough-going God-centredness. Through loss to gain is the first principle of Christian morals. But cross-bearing is also a vivification, a rising again to newness of life. From Christ to the Christian the pattern of death and resurrection is transmitted, first in the sacrament of baptism and then in that life of baptismal regeneration which St Paul has expressed in pregnant phrases: "I die daily" and "No longer I but Christ liveth in me." [1]

A second general principle is that the priesthood of the whole Church is the necessary complement to the ministerial priesthood of the bishops and presbyters. The ministerial priesthood sets men apart for those special functions which Christ gave to his apostles and makes them the ministers of the Word and Sacraments, the pastors, evangelists, and teachers of the flock, the guardians of the faith and worship of the Church. Their ministry is in and for the believing and worshipping Church, though it has also a mission to those who are not yet aware of their redemption by Christ. But it is the Church as a whole, clergy and laity together, who have to let their light shine before men and to be the leaven, witnessing by their common life to Christ and his saving work. Even on the purely practical level, and apart from theological theory, to do this wherever men and women live their daily lives and do their daily work is manifestly impossible for that tiny minority of Christians who are in holy orders. In the twelfth chapter of 1 Corinthians St Paul has given classic expression to the "diversities of workings" required for the full impact of the Church upon the world. His rhetorical questions, Are all apostles? Are

[1] 1 Cor. 15. 31; Gal. 2. 20. Cf. also 2 Cor. 4. 10, 5. 17.

all prophets? Are all teachers?, are telling reminders of the common responsibility of the whole body, no less than of the special functions of the apostolic ministry.

Thirdly, we must beware of thinking that the priesthood of all believers is exercised only in those areas of human life which are commonly spoken of as religious, or spiritual, or ecclesiastical. "A keen churchman" is a phrase often used in an unduly limited sense. In more senses than one Christianity is emphatically a lay religion. We do, indeed, need a great variety of assistance, given by a great number of people, in maintaining the work and worship of the dioceses and parishes and in conducting the manifold charitable enterprises carried on under the auspices of the Church. The people who give such services deserve unstinted gratitude; and the affectation of superiority and mild amusement sometimes displayed by superior persons in speaking of those who help with the parochial routine is one of the meanest kinds of snobbery. But it is also true that "church work" should be thought of as extending far beyond the sacristy and the choir, the Sunday School and the parish hall. It is not necessary to serve at the altar or sing in the choir, to teach in Sunday School, or distribute parish magazines in order to do "church work". It may be doubted whether Mr T. S. Eliot has done any of these things; but to write *Murder in the Cathedral* is just as much "church work". I know an eminent Christian philosopher who does serve at the altar, but his serving at the altar is no more an exercise of baptismal priesthood than his critical and constructive philosophical thinking. Perhaps it is less so, for he is not always strictly punctual in his attendance at the Holy Eucharist.

"The world is my parish", said John Wesley. That was an exaggeration, no doubt a pardonable one, on the lips of one man, however eminent as a Christian preacher, but it is strictly true of the priestly community of the Christians. They have to present Christ and the Gospel not only to all men but also to every kind of grouping. In every social institution, in every ideological or economic structure the Christian way must be shown, the Christian critique must be heard. The most urgent need of our time is that this should be done with far greater vigour and militancy by the rank and file of the Church. For the Church is not only the ark of salvation. It is the Body of Christ, and therefore the living instrument of the eternal wisdom and the fullness of him who filleth all things. The Lord has set his Church in the world both for the conversion of individuals and for the refashioning, in truth and charity, of all the collectivities that organize the social life of mankind.

St Paul states this very clearly. He is concerned not only with the salvation of this or that Jew or Gentile who may be converted to the Faith. He writes in the Epistle to the Romans of God's purpose for "all Israel" and of the providential design in the calling of the Gentiles as the way by which this saving of Israel is to be accomplished. The function of the Church, as nucleus and organ of the kingdom of God, inherently includes this dual approach to what we call "evangelism". We have to do with the liberation of the individual soul, seeking salvation, and with the redemption of society, the "healing of the nations".

We cannot afford to neglect either task. The conversion of individuals is required because every man, woman, and child is a unique creature of God, a person who is an end and not a means. Christ's parables of the lost sheep and the lost coin show beyond possibility of doubt that God will not allow us to abandon an individual concern for individuals. God is not a politician aiming at the crowd or the majority.

He is no remote bureaucrat operating upon people in the mass from behind a screen of card-indexes and statistical records. Yet at the same time the Christian religion is not confined to "private life". It seeks to redeem man in all the complexity of his social being. No man is a purely private individual. His relations with his fellows, on every level, economic, political, international, are integral to his existence. The more far-reaching of these relations cry out for redemption no less than every man's immediate relations with his own family, his friends, and his next door neighbour. What used to be called "the social gospel" is somewhat out of fashion to-day, largely because it was too often associated with opinions which both on historical and on theological grounds have deservedly been rejected. Nevertheless, the Gospel is directed to man in society as well as to man in the inner citadel of his individual separateness. The full range of the Church's mission to the world cannot be appreciated unless both objectives are taken with full seriousness.

6

THE APOSTOLATE OF THE LAITY

The previous chapter sketched in the outlines of "the priesthood of all believers", the corporate priesthood of the Church, which stands in the world of men mediating the Gospel in worship and work. We were concerned with the New Testament foundations of this truth about the Church and with a few guiding principles which emerged from the New Testament material. Now I want to expand the subject of baptismal priesthood a little further, mainly by a few suggestions or reminders of some practical forms in which that priesthood is expressed.

Let me say first that the apostolate of the laity is a rational implication of deep-rooted theological truths about Christ and his mystical Body. It is not a piece of loose rhetoric. Nor is it a grandiloquent way of saying that we ought to be kind to one another. Nor again is it a commission to go about in a haze of revivalist emotion asking all and sundry whether they are saved. Christ's redemptive work involved a great deal more than the proclamation of ethical generalities and the awakening of religious emotions. So too, with his Church. For effective Christianity we have to mobilize all the powers of mind and will in an enterprise that taxes them to the full. We need to have a strong and definite body of theological convictions firmly articulated and well thought out, as well as the moral graces of charity and patience. That means study and intellectual effort. Then again, we must take the life of prayer seriously. Otherwise our Christianity becomes just one more ideology, a thing only for argument and propaganda and all manner of stunts. We must be thorough and businesslike in our plans of campaign, the strategy and tactics of the Christian warfare. Conviction without bigotry, charity without sloppiness, zeal without fanaticism: these are not easy of achievement, but we have to try.

There are two New Testament images which we may profitably use to organize our thinking about the lay apostolate. They are light and leaven.[1]

Christ is the light of the world, and he said that his disciples were the light of the world. So the Church exists to bring the light of the Gospel to bear upon the obscurities and confusion of human life. Seen from this angle the Church stands apart from the world and acts upon it from without. It has to maintain itself as the source of light, to be watchful against anything that might dim the radiance of Christ and his truth. It has to do this not only for its own sake but also for the world. In other words the Church, which cannot stop short with its own self-development, has to cherish its own inner life of faith and worship in order that it may convey light. The light is Christ; not some self-generated human phosphorescence but the heavenly light of the divine Word. Fidelity to Christ, with all that this implies both intellectually and morally, is the first essential of the apostolate.

The second image, the leaven, suggests a complementary mode of action. Now we have an image not of invasion from without, as of light striking upon dark places, but of a more secret operation from within. The Christians have thus a dual task. In part it is to stand aside from the world, to

[1] Matt. 5. 14, 13. 33.

maintain their city set upon the hill as the place where the divine light may shine unobscured and go out to overthrow the darkness. In part it is to penetrate the world and bring about a social transformation from within. As the incarnate Lord accepted the conditions of human life, so that the redemptive action of God was not a dazzling theophany but the life of Jesus, Mary's son, among peasants and fishermen; so the Christians have to go into the world, into politics and government, business and industry, as artists or scientists, factory workers or film stars, housewives or haberdashers, in every department of man's activity. Thus, quietly and often secretly and silently they have to bring the Christian ferment into the whole life of man.

With these two images in mind, we can briefly check over some of the ways in which the lay apostolate will find its practical fulfilment. I will borrow a word much used in connection with the striking revival that is going on in the French Church to-day, the word "militant". How shall we describe the Christian militant? With what resources must he be equipped and by what activities will his Christianity declare itself?

I have already indicated two items of his—or her—equipment. He must have some theological grounding; and he must practise the life of prayer. Some theological grounding, for he cannot do his work of witness by the light of nature and the Bible lessons he was given, or not given, when he was at school. The idea that theology is for clergymen only will not do. It is an impossible notion in these days, when Christians can take nothing for granted; when sheer ignorance of Christian doctrine or grotesque caricatures of it are widespread and when atheism, scientific humanism, and the like are propagated by men of skill and determination, men who are willing to take great pains to master their briefs. Instructed Christians are more than ever needed to meet this attack. This is not to say that the Christian factory worker or housewife must be put through the studies proper to an honours degree in theology or delve deep into the history of Christian doctrine. They need not know whether Nestorius or someone else was the real author of Nestorianism or decide whether Archbishop Cranmer was a Zwinglian. But as every member of the Communist party must have, or be prepared to acquire, a good working knowledge of what Communism means, so the Christian militant will seek to acquire a good working knowledge of what he affirms when he recites the Nicene creed. It is not a question of high scholarship, historical learning, or theological subtlety. These things inevitably are for a small minority. Nor again ought we to expect Everyman to be able to stand on platforms or in pulpits or deliver lectures on apologetics. But some attempt to study the Faith at however elementary a level, and to apply our minds to it, is not too much to ask. And all the more so, the more educational advantages we have had.

Our Christian militant will, then, avail himself of such opportunities of adult religious education as may be open to him. Then he will learn to practise, with perseverance and intelligent care, the great art of prayer, both liturgical and private. A real attempt to enter into the meaning of the Liturgy is indispensable for anyone who takes his religious profession seriously; so, too, is some kind of meditation or devotional Bible study. There are two compelling reasons for this. First, we exist for God; and prayer, the ascent of the mind to God, is the recognition of this, the deepest truth about men. Secondly, the kind of Christian activism which claims that it is sufficient to worship God by daily work and kindliness in human relationships deludes itself, because it begins at the end. No doubt, a perfect saint, if there were such a person, might reach such a perfect transmutation of life into worship. Most of us are a very long way from that perfection and need the regular and habitual practices of devotion, if our daily lives are not to fade into secularism and the most banal kind of conventionality.

Next, our Christian militant will consider how greatly he needs close association and co-operation with others. The lone-wolf Christian cannot get very far, and he exposes himself to gratuitous difficulties and dangers. Co-operation both with the clergy and with other lay Christians is a condition of any effective apostolate, as it is also a safeguard for the individual. All Christian history shows the importance of the group round a leader. This appears in such central institutions of the Church as the parish and the monastery and in the innumerable enterprises, cultural, philanthropic, evangelistic, and what not, which Christian zeal has launched upon the world. To associate in cells and groups, to work as a member of a team, is not only to find the strength of mutual support; it greatly increases the force of the Christian impact. This has become more than ever clear in the circumstances of modern life. To-day a more or less dechristianized society exercises an enormous adverse pressure upon the individual Christian, who as a Christian can never be content to float with the tide of mass opinion but finds tremendous forces working against him.

The witness, we must add, remains in a very real sense individual witness. The Christian militant, in the works or the office, on the land or in the forces, wherever he may find himself, has to act as an individual, whether it be by positive action or by protest and refusal. But group fellowship enormously strengthens him and should be the normal background. The same applies to his contribution to the evangelistic work of his parish church in his own home district, no less than to his efforts to be loyal to Christ and his Church among his companions at work. A group of Christian families, for example, can do a great deal, both in direct evangelistic work and by the powerful effect of a common life in Christian charity, to leaven the dechristianized lump in their immediate neighbourhood.

It is hardly necessary to do more than mention the need for Christians to take an effective share in public life, both local and national. Stated in these general terms, the need is obvious and the merest commonplace. Yet the commonplace conceals some very delicate problems: in particular, the problem of the Christian in politics and particularly in party politics.

Nothing is more certain than that the Christian is involved, willy-nilly, in the political life of his country and cannot withdraw into some ivory tower above the battle. But what is the nature of this involvement? For many, if not most Christians in this country the answer has seemed to be that he should support one or other political party, as the only practical way of political action. Certainly the main political parties need a strong Christian element. And the fact that this procedure splits the Christians into opposing camps does not seem to matter very much, the British party system being what it is. The old jibes "the Church of England the Conservative party at prayer" and "court chaplains to King Demos" fall rather flat in these days, when the two major parties have so much in common, within the general framework of the democratic Welfare State, and when those of any religion or none unite within either party for common secular ends. No one to-day can reasonably say that a churchman is grinding the faces of the poor, if he votes Conservative, or is siding with bloody

revolution, if he votes Labour. More or less private enterprise, more or less State control are questions that hardly
raise any fundamental issues of Christian principle. The
Christian may well feel free to use his own judgement on
what are essentially questions of method and to adopt
whatever political programme seems to him most service-
able for the common good. Christianity as such is not
committed either to "capitalism", in its regulated modern
form, or to State collectivism. What it is opposed to in
principle is any form of totalitarianism, whether of the
right or of the left, because totalitarianism denies the
supremacy of God's law over the laws of the State. And it
has to be remembered that totalitarianism can mask itself
with democratic forms and parliamentary institutions and
does not need an overt despotism to enforce its will.

Christians in other countries have often met the political
problem by means of a separate party organization. Every-
one has heard of Christian Democrats and the M.R.P. and
some may have asked themselves whether this is the right
solution of the problem. Since neither capitalism nor
State Socialism nor Communism is to be identified simply
with Christianity on its political side, should we form a
separate Christian party as the only logical alternative to
the hopeless view that Christianity has nothing to do with
politics? Or shall we accept the common mind of English
Christians that a separate Christian party creates more
difficulties than it solves and is no way out? The situation
in our own country does not suggest to most of us that a
Christian party is the only effective way of avoiding that
escapism which turns Christianity into a private piety with
nothing to say about man's social welfare here on earth.

If I have thrown out points for discussion rather than
attempted to answer the question, what is the layman to do,

it is not only because space forbids any longer treatment of this matter. There is another reason. I do not think history encourages us to suppose that the clergy can, or should, relieve the laity of their responsibility in this business of political action. It is essential that the Christian layman should exercise the liberty of the Christian man and reach his own free and responsible decision. I would add only one further reflection. The problems thus briefly touched upon in these last few paragraphs have great importance in practice and they go very deep. For they are rooted in the age-long difficulty, plainly visible on every page of Christian history, of how best to combine Christian discipleship with secular citizenship in "the kingdoms of this world". The Church and State question is obviously too big for discussion here; but it is inescapable. It is something our Christian militant cannot shirk in practice, any more than the theologian can escape it in theory. For, whether he be conservative, socialist, or independent, the Christian's political decisions are to be seen as an integral part of his apostolate. In reaching these decisions it may be that, for our practice here and now in this present year of grace, we have to be content with the conventional advice to take a leaf out of the Fabian book and adopt the policy of permeating the existing parties from within. It may be that it is possible to devise some other way. What we cannot do is just wash our hands of the matter and turn our religion into a private devotional satisfaction. We have to render unto Caesar the things that are Caesar's.

I have touched—very lightly and briefly, but that is inevitable—upon Christian action in the places where men and women live and work, and in the political life of the community. But the scope and variety of our responsibility are still wider. Great tracts of the area of that responsibility have not even been mentioned. We have so far said nothing of such outstanding tasks as the Christian mission to the heathen, the work of Christian education, the work of promoting external unity among Christians. These, too, are the proper field for the lay apostolate, concerns of the whole Church, not of the clergy alone. We have a fine heritage of lay activity in the missionary societies of the Church of England, in the schools and universities and in the parishes. It is a heritage that needs to be taken up and developed by an increasing number of churchpeople, as the growing and changing problems of our own day clamour for Christian solution. In the life of the British people to-day there is an ever-growing tendency towards State action and reliance upon it for all sorts of benefits, social security, free education, free health services, and so on. For Christians this ought to be a stimulus; it must not be a narcotic, lulling into inactivity the healthy impulses towards community service. It ought to mean greater freedom and a wider range of opportunity for those Christian activities which no State can undertake. The field for initiative and voluntary service remains wide open in the life of the Church. Here the Christian should be more than ever alert and enterprising. By his profession he is bound to the service of Christ and the Gospel. But indirectly he will also be doing valuable service to the community generally. For the Welfare State is a good servant but a bad master. The benefits it confers may induce—it is not a fanciful supposition—an essentially servile and most disastrous frame of mind which looks to a paternal government for everything and devoutly believes that it is more blessed to receive than to give. Initiative, self-help, voluntary effort, of course, are not dead in contemporary society; but Christians can do much to maintain them in vigorous life and they have their own compelling reasons for setting an example, both as Christians and as citizens.

The field of opportunity that we have thus hastily surveyed is very wide. Indeed, the spaciousness and splendour of the Christian vocation grows with the years. So some specialization is inevitable. We cannot all do everything. That is no loss, provided that the general body of the Christian laity is engaged and does not leave these concerns to a few enthusiasts. The ground can be covered, if there are enough people to lend a hand.

The conclusion of the matter is plain enough and the writer of this book may be permitted to state it in a direct and practical form. Every reader of these pages would find it a profitable exercise, and not least in Lent, to examine himself or herself on the contribution he or she is making, in one or other part of the vast area we have surveyed, to the impact upon the world of the holy people of God.

7

HOMO EUCHARISTICUS

We have been reviewing the meaning of priesthood and sacrifice and trying to see how deep these ideas go into the New Testament presentation of Christ and the Gospel. They are not, perhaps, very popular ideas. Even among Christians they are to many still the object of grave suspicion. Yet, as I have tried to show, they deserve to be rescued from the fog of prejudice and denominational feuds in which they have been plunged for some four hundred years. They deserve it on their intrinsic merits, because they are, as we have seen, genuinely biblical and Christian ideas, necessary for a truly historical understanding of the Christian Faith. Just as in the last thirty or forty years the idea of the Church has come back into the thinking of all serious theologians in all the main Christian traditions, so we may hope that the idea of priesthood will come back and be seen as equally important and truly evangelical. For priesthood is just as much *there*, present and operative in the biblical material, as is the idea of the Church.

There is another reason why we should strive for the frank and full recognition of priesthood and sacrifice in the Gospel. Both in the history of mankind generally, and in the biblical revelation, these terms belong to the language of worship. And the idea of worship takes us to the fundamental purpose both of the creation of man by Almighty God and of the redemption of man by the Incarnation of the

Word. For the biblical understanding of man is that he exists not to please himself nor even to please his neighbour but to do the will of God; in the words that have been the recurring motif of this book "to offer his body as a living sacrifice, holy, acceptable to God, which is his spiritual [or rational] worship". This is the truth upon which our Lord placed the seal of his supreme authority when he taught that the first and great commandment is to love God. It is to enable man to do this that the Son of Man was made man, lived, died, rose again, and sent the Holy Spirit upon his redeemed brethren.

All this is, of course, meaningless and infuriating to the Marxist and the secularist, for whom man is anything but the priest of God. Nothing, however, is more distinctively and decisively the Christian interpretation of the mystery of man's existence. The reality of God, the supreme authority of God, his will, his law, his love, over all human concerns whatsoever—these are the foundations of that Christian *philosophia perennis* which negates every form of secularism and naturalism. Man exists for God and in the last analysis for nothing else.

Hence it follows that worship is man's primary function and duty. Worship has its roots in the recognition of God's sovereignty and of man's creaturely status and essential dependence. This dependence blossoms in the Christian revelation into a voluntary and loving co-operation with the divine love, made possible for us by our incorporation into the mystical Body of Christ, the only begotten Son of God. This co-operation is fully ethical in character, but morality by itself is not enough. An impersonal moral law, a code of good behaviour, virtue, duty, or any other abstraction, is only a sophisticated kind of idol. Salvation by man's own efforts after virtuous conduct is certainly not the meaning of the Christian religion. The real heart of the matter is worship of the living God. That is the specific *differentia* of a religious understanding of existence and *a fortiori* of the Christian Faith.

Two qualities of worship stand out as primary. In the first place, worship is made possible only as a response to the initiative of God in Christ. This does not mean that the natural religions of mankind are a mere sham, for God has never left himself without witness and in every sincere effort after worship there is some grace of God at work, some blundering and imperfect feeling after the truth in some hearts. Worship "in Christ" is the fulfilment of all this. Secondly, worship fully understood is nothing less than the total offering of the self in a life of loving obedience to the ethical demands of Christ, the revealer of God and the truth incarnate. There is no possibility for the Christian of a ritual cultus which is a *substitute* for the good life. That was decided once for all by the prophets of Israel long ago, by Amos, Hosea, Micah, Isaiah eight hundred years before the Incarnation. Nevertheless, if a truly God-centred ordering of everything in human life is to be maintained in practice, it must of necessity have a focus of attention in acts of cultus, ritual actions which constantly correct and enforce man's response to God. As St Thomas Aquinas teaches, God does not need our positive acts of cultus, our churchgoing and our private devotions. It is we who need them, we who cannot, in the long run, preserve the worship of our lives without the worship of our lips. Our Lord himself has provided us with these necessities by giving us the Holy Eucharist and the Lord's Prayer.

The Eucharist is at one and the same time the focus of worship and the inspiration and control of the good life. The traditional structure of the Liturgy is the mirror in which we see the form and fashion of what that life should be.

The central eucharistic action begins at the offertory. There we see men bringing their lives and works as an offering to God. The gifts of bread and wine, these fruits of man's labour on the products of the earth, are the fitting symbols of that will to worship which is the true orientation of all human activity. Yet man, the sinner, cannot of himself offer an acceptable worship. His sin defiles his offering. Only the Son of Man, Jesus Christ, has offered acceptably a pure offering. It is only as we men are brought into union with him in his new humanity that we can share his filial obedience and so worship God aright. So it is that, in answer to the Church's prayer made in Christ's name, God the Father makes our symbols of bread and wine the Body and Blood of Christ, the new man, and unites us sacramentally to the perfect oblation. The consecration leads to communion; and that communion is in a sacrifice, the one, true, pure, immortal sacrifice presented in the heavenly order by our great High Priest and presented sacramentally by the same High Priest at earthly altars through the ministry of human priests, ministering in and for the priestly Church.

We see in the drama of the Eucharist the whole pattern of human life as it should be: redeemed humanity in and with Christ, its redeemer, being brought as an offering of love to the Father. Into that oblation we enter in the most intimate and personal way. For individually, one by one, we receive in Holy Communion the very instruments wherewith the incarnate Lord, in his divine humanity, made his perfect and culminating act of obedience to his Father—his own Body and Blood. In that ineffable union we worship, as without it we cannot worship in spirit and in truth.

What is thus done focally and in a divinely ordered supernatural mystery at the table of the Lord has then to flow out into the life of every day. It has to sweep into its current the thoughts, words, and works of every man, turning them from selfish and transient satisfactions into the stuff of sacrificial worship and filial obedience. Sinful man, as the Christian religion sees, is to become eucharistic man.

He has tried to shape himself on many other models. In the modern world of the last half millennium he has seen himself in several distorting mirrors. He has tried to be economic man, with the development of large-scale capitalist industry, the technological exploitation of natural resources, increasing urbanization, and the new opportunities of unheard-of wealth and material comfort. Again, he has seen himself as a kind of super-man of godlike power and self-sufficiency. The Renaissance glorification of man's good opinion of himself, the romantic perfectionism of Rousseau, the magical spells of scientific techniques accumulating in his hands at a furious pace—all this combined to make him dizzy with the intoxication of power and the illusion of autonomy. These notions still exercise great sway in our contemporary world. They are being partly countered, partly reinforced, by the twentieth-century new model, Soviet man, conditioned from birth by the twin despotisms of economic determinism and the party machine.

So we plunge about from one notion of man to another in a self-assurance that persists, though it is somewhat clouded to-day by hydrogen-bomb explosions. It remains the Church's task to set forth eucharistic man, man the worshipper, as against any and every naturalistic or secular reading of human nature.

This supernaturalism will, of course, mean that we shall be told that Christians are looking backwards to a long-dead past, to the ideas of a pre-scientific age. We have, indeed, to be careful not to indulge in any sentimental medievalism or any kind of reactionary or escapist antics. But we need feel no compunction about reasserting a theological interpretation of man in an age of science. Science, in any intelligent use of that term, has produced nothing to invalidate the belief in "God the Father who hath made me and all the world, God the Son who hath redeemed me and all mankind, God the Holy Ghost who sanctifieth me and all the elect people of God". These ultimates are not displaced by any extension of natural knowledge of the created universe, by a more exact understanding of the processes by which it has reached its present form or of the mechanisms of its energy-systems. They are as compatible with quantum-theory as with Newtonian physics, with modern cosmologies as with the elaborate ingenuity of Ptolemaic astronomy, with an evolutionary biology as with any other.

The troubles of our age of science and of the machine do not lie either with the science or the machine. We do not go to the Devil because we use artificial fertilizers or because the conveyor-belt has supplanted the handicraftsman. The peril we are in lies elsewhere. It lies where St Paul saw it. As he surveyed the no less corrupt civilization of his own day and delivered his classic indictment in the first chapter of the Epistle to the Romans, he put his finger on the spot when he spoke of that "reprobate mind" which proceeds from men's refusal to "have God in their knowledge". The root of the matter is still the same. It is what the moral theologian calls the sin of pride, that ultimate lie by which man spoils everything, as he denies his own essential nature as creature, wholly dependent upon his Creator.

The true humility is the recognition of this dependence. As man "comes to himself" and returns to his Father by the grace of our Lord Jesus Christ, he recovers his own proper place in the created order. Once more he can be the priest of nature, the vicegerent of God in the terrestrial setting of his life in time. Inorganic matter, the forces of nature, the animal creation are his to use; but they are his conditionally. The condition is always that he uses them for God, whose agent he is, and not as their absolute master with unlimited freedom to decide what uses he will make of them. He is a mediator, not an absolute monarch. He is bound by the law of God, whose writ runs everywhere. Within these limits he exercises his royal priesthood. It is royal because man stands highest among earthly creatures, highest in his nature and in his power. It is priesthood because man's function is ministerial and mediatorial, as the Eden picture of Adam the gardener presents him.

"What is man, that thou art mindful of him, and the son of man, that thou visitest him? Thou madest him lower than the angels to crown him with glory and worship. Thou makest him to have dominion of the works of thy hands." In the psalmist's words we can find the aptest summary of man's true character and status; and in the opening words of the eighth psalm, "O Lord our governor, how excellent is thy Name in all the world", that necessary, overruling truth which conditions all that the human creature can ever do or be.

"Thou shalt worship the Lord thy God and him only shalt thou serve." So the tempted Son of Man said to the Devil in the wilderness. In that worship and that service Christ has made finally known to us the true fulfilment of man on this earth and in eternity.

So our brief study of the royal priesthood shapes for us a vision of man that is not at the mercy of passing intellectual fashions but is rooted in the revealed purpose of man's Creator. That purpose is made known to us in Holy Scripture and these chapters have been little more than meditations upon some of those biblical themes which give the Bible its underlying unity. Yet what emerges is not just a series of studies in an ancient book, but a release from the illusions and frustrations that bedevil contemporary society. The Christian doctrine of man has an unaging freshness and relevance. It is nearly two thousand years old but it remains perennially satisfying and stimulating. We who are Christians should have the strength of our convictions. We have a paramount duty to present this truth about man as something more than a mere alternative to secularist ideas; to present it as a real liberation of mankind from the sterile and cramping ideologies of what is called the "post-Christian" world. It is high time that the Christians knew their strength and took the offensive. In the biblical pattern of the royal priesthood they have the strategical plan for that attack. To recover our hold on the allegiance of the now dechristianized masses we must have a doctrine of man as well as a doctrine of God. We need to realize afresh and to assert with a new conviction that only as man is seen in the light of the Christian revelation of God's redeeming act in Christ can man's "place in nature" and his life in community be given their true perspective and their true fulfilment.

A TALE OF TWO CITIES

The Christian is a citizen of two cities. He came to his baptism a member of an earthly family, a citizen of an earthly nation; and he went from the font still a member of both the family and the nation. But baptism made him a citizen of the eternal city of the children of God and gave him a wholly new allegiance to another family and another sovereign. Throughout his life he will have this dual allegiance.

At first sight it might seem a desperate situation, for the two centres of his loyalty are incommensurable and some-times—so experience teaches—they are incompatible one with the other. For consider what is involved.

The earthly city—let us call it Terrena—enforces upon its subjects a mode of life of absorbing interest and diversity. But there is a dark side to it. It is marred through and through by sin (our Christian has to know what that word means) and it is set inexorably within a framework of limitations. The first limitation, obviously, is that of time. A man has a half-century or so of adult life, if he escapes the hazards of war, disease, and accident. Then death ends his earthly career. During these years on earth he is occupied from day to day in the task of making a living, which takes most of his energies. He has his private life, in his own home and among his friends, for such part of his days as remains when the day's work is done. He has to fulfil his citizen duties. He may have cultural interests, hobbies, games, and so on to add to the list of his activities. In all these ways he is able to live a full and interesting life. But it is short, and the end is certain.

A second limitation is that the whole of this life cycle—its laws and institutions, its conventions of behaviour, and its scale of values—is devoted to the maintenance of Terrenian existence. Economic necessity, the biological urges of self-preservation and reproduction, the social and cultural values of earthly existence are the controlling forces. They compel a concentration of thought and will and effort upon those things that make life on earth possible and desirable. For Terrena has nothing more to give. It knows no other objective. True, the welfare of future generations is included in the values it commends; but for the individual himself there is nothing beyond the limits of his earthly span. He will not live to see the fruits of what he may have done to improve the conditions of life for posterity.

Philosophers throughout the ages have moralized upon this life of man on earth. According to their temperaments, they have either bewailed the vanity of human wishes, with Ecclesiastes, or, with Lucretius, they have urged men to accept the banquet of life, and leave it like a satisfied guest who asks no more. In either case Terrena is a city of men who will inevitably be robbed of any further participation in Terrenian existence.

But the Christian is made by baptism a citizen of another country—Urania, the City of God. Here the scale of values is very different. For now there is the dimension of eternity to give a wholly new meaning to human life. Now life on earth is only an episode. Its values are relative to something beyond itself. The passage through this world is a pilgrimage to another city whose citizens do not cease to be after their three score years and ten. For the death of the body does not close the story. Death is indeed a momentous crisis, but it is a crisis of transition, a turning point in a life that is not earthbound. Now not self, nor even neighbour, but God is the centre towards whom in the last analysis every thought and word and act must be directed. Communion with God, prayer, penitence, adoration, the submission of every vital activity to the rule of God have now to assume control, and to make the over-all pattern of the life in Christ which is eternal life.

How are these two orders of existence to be unified? The question covers the whole moral life of the Christian. Neither order can just be set aside. It is not a question of choosing between them. The second can only be for those who are born into the first. Nor can Urania be disregarded until Terrenian life is ending, for the two must somehow synchronize; otherwise we are in peril of losing our Uranian citizenship altogether. Somehow they have to be brought into a single focus. How is that to be done?

Part of the Christian answer is the theme of this book. In the royal priesthood of the people of God we have the reconciling principle that we need. With this to guide us, we see that man is here on earth to exercise a mediatory office, as a responsible steward of the earthly riches entrusted to him. He is never to make them an end in themselves or to consider himself their absolute owner. But neither is he to shirk the responsibility of using them rightly; and "rightly" means for the glory of God and, by consequence, for the purposes of man's own eternal welfare. The corrupting forces of sin will not allow him to do this, and he needs God's redeeming act to free him from the tyranny of evil. In Christ he receives his liberation and in Christ he returns to his priestly and mediatorial status. He has to be otherworldly in order that he can be, in the only right sense of the word, this-worldly.

Secular humanism, being limited to this world, can find no meaning in man's existence. It can only bid him make the best of a bad job, finding what satisfactions, noble or ignoble, are available to him, while time and health and opportunity permit. Christian humanism can do better than that. It sets the highest value on this life, because it sees how important and meaningful it is in the divine plan. Here man both undergoes his probation for eternity and exercises his ministry of mediation. All the concerns of this world take on a new and splendid dignity because they are a God-given opportunity for learning how to worship. The glory that shall be is beyond our present comprehending or imagining; but our faith is content to see through a glass, darkly, that it is the glory of eternal fellowship with God in the community of the redeemed with angels and archangels and all the company of heaven. Christ the priest sends his ministerial priests to build up that faith, to be the sacramental ministers of divine grace, to offer the sacrifice of praise and thanksgiving in and for the priestly body. The priestly body, knowing itself to be what it is as it meets for the eucharistic sacrifice, has its sins forgiven, its eyes enlightened, its will renewed, that it may go back into the world that God made, the world in which he has set his sons for a time that they may glorify him both here and hereafter.

PART II

The Inner Life of the Priest

INTRODUCTORY NOTE

Ministerial priesthood has been for centuries one of the learned professions. As such it has its appropriate training and techniques. It can be professionally assessed as a form of service to the community comparable to that of the doctor or teacher. Like all professions it is more than just a way of earning one's living or carrying out certain specified duties.

But it is unlike other professions in that it calls for an unusual degree of personal commitment, and that in two main ways.

Once a priest, always a priest. Priesthood cannot be laid aside out of office hours or exchanged at will for some other career. It is a lifelong dedication made under vow at the time of ordination, comparable in this respect to Christian marriage or solemn profession in a religious community. Nothing but the gravest and most compelling reasons can dispense from the priest's vows.

Secondly, priesthood unites in a special degree an interior discipline to its outward activities. It is a spiritual life to be lived even more than a varied and exacting round of services to be rendered. All professions have their ethical standards, to which those who practise them are expected to conform. But this profession links professional work with a reference to the supernatural order more intimate and more thoroughly pervasive than any other.

Hence the spiritual life of the priest is of the *esse* of his vocation. His ministry of the Word and the Sacraments can never be merely a trade, an external manipulation of spiritual goods; it must of necessity be a witness to what he himself is using as the daily sustenance of his own life at its deepest levels. The pages that follow are offered to my brethren of the clergy as an attempt to analyse, simply and shortly, the ways in which this understanding of ministerial priesthood may be given practical form.

8

ASCENSIO MENTIS AD DEUM

"Will you be diligent in prayers, and in reading of the holy
Scriptures, and in such studies as help to the knowledge of
the same, laying aside the study of the world and the flesh?"
In this question, addressed by the bishop to every Anglican
candidate for the priesthood, the basic principles of the
priest's vocation are summarized in pithy, memorable
phrases. It is with these principles that our study of priesthood finds its first point of entry.

1

Prayer, study, the relation between the two: here is the
essential triad, here the three strands out of which the tex-
ture of the priestly life is woven. In order to practise that
life, the priest must understand and faithfully apply these
principles, because in no other way can he put first things
first and observe due proportion in his aims and activities.
It is true that he is a man speaking to other men: as an
evangelist and a pastor, a minister of sacramental grace
and a physician of souls, he is constantly active in the service
of his fellows. But what he has to give is not some self-
generated wisdom invented by himself; it is a revelation of
truth and a saving power, mediated through him from the
unsearchable riches of Christ. It is before all else a witness,
bearing testimony to what comes from above, from the

manifold wisdom of God. Inevitably, therefore, if his ministerial priesthood is to have its authentic content, he is committed, in the first place, to the total submission of his own thought and his own life to the control of divine truth. If he is to minister to men, it is above all things necessary that he should be a man of God. No professional techniques, no powers of "leadership", no oratorical or administrative gifts can take the place of this *unum necessarium*.

The priest cannot acquire this primary qualification once for all, like a little boy learning to do up his own buttons, and then take it for granted while he plunges into practical activities. Rather he is bound to a progressive understanding and a progressive application of divine things; and this is the work of a lifetime. Here there is always something more to learn and to do. The deepest spirituality is an endless docility, always aware of the fathomless riches still to be explored, and the saint is ever in his own eyes not a master but a learner in the school of the divine wisdom. As Walter Hilton says,[1] "the service of God is the noblest of all crafts"; and whereas the mere apprentice in a very simple craft may become proficient from the start, the noblest craft demands long and sustained attention, that "diligence" which the ordinand is to promise.

For the purposes of this chapter we can be well content with a familiar definition of prayer. From at least the time of St John Damascene it has been excellently defined as the ascent of the mind to God. The definition is valuable not least because of its noble generality. By "mind" in this context we do not mean the instrument of mere discursive reasoning, but rather the whole nature of man under the control of those higher spiritual qualities which lift him above the animal level. In so turning all the powers of the

[1] *Ladder of Perfection*, ii, 19.

soul Godwards we have a wide liberty. We are not restricted to a limited number of techniques or formed methods, nor to set times and places. We must, indeed, have techniques and methods. Prayer is not a vague mooning or day-dreaming. Even when it is at its most formless—as on occasion it quite rightly is—a blind and dumb contemplative prayer rests both upon an ordered body of religious convictions and upon a religious practice which includes the methodical use of forms of prayer, in the Liturgy and in private devotion. But all methods are but aids to prayer; they are the scaffolding rather than the edifice itself. Prayer itself is, or aims at being, a constant state, that habitual God-centredness, in loving, filial obedience, which is the true fulfilment of man's nature. The ascent of the mind to God, faithfully cultivated both in set times of ordered religious exercises and in the increasingly fruitful "practice of the presence of God", has endless variety and an almost limitless freedom. The ways of communion with God can vary from the intricate ceremonial pattern of pontifical High Mass to the old woman "peeling her potatoes to the glory of God". All are good ways.

It is within the large freedom of this definition of prayer that we have to see the close connection that exists between the two parts of the priest's vow: to be diligent in prayer and to be diligent in study. The heart of the matter may be expressed thus: the priest's prayer must be theological and his theology must be turned into prayer.

2

The priest's prayer must be theological. What does that mean?

The meaning depends upon a truth that is quite simple and that issues from the very foundations of the Christian Faith. The priest is concerned with God, and with God's revelation of himself. He is not ordained to expound his own beautiful thoughts about religion and morals. He is ordained to bear witness—a witness in word, deed, and suffering—to a unique divine revelation. That revelation must master him; it must shape his thinking, control his action, direct his will. St Paul did not hesitate to call himself "the slave of Christ", and those who stand in the apostolic succession and are entrusted with the apostolic ministry are in the like happy state. In such a service, the priest must continually submit himself, with a glad and zestful submission, to theology, to the discipline of studying the revelation of God in Christ, as it is given to him in the Bible, the Liturgy, and the Church. It is in that most fundamental and most important sense that he must be *theologos*, a theologian.

It is inevitable that, after well-nigh two thousand years of Christian thought, the word "theology" should suggest a vast accumulation of learning, and that by a "theologian" we should commonly mean one who is deeply versed in the multitudinous detail of what men have said and written about the mysteries of the Faith in previous ages. True, no man can master the whole, and academic study of theology is team work, carried on by specialists in one or other field within the immense area to be explored. Such specialization is necessary, but it has the unfortunate result of still further restricting the popular image of the theologian; he appears as the *savant* who knows more and more about less and less. The ordinand as an undergraduate at the university, and as a theological college student, will gain some acquaintance with this world of theological scholarship, and it is a quite indispensable part of his training. More than that, it is eminently desirable that he should keep up his academic studies after his ordination. Yet the busy parish priest, immersed in the manifold duties of an active ministry, has neither the time nor the facilities for the scholarship proper to the occupant of a theological chair in a university. He ought, indeed, to read as many as he can of the more important books written by the academic theologians, for there he will find the researches of many specialist scholars critically assessed and co-ordinated. Only by such reading can he keep his mind theologically awake. For if theology is not a preserve for a few academic specialists, neither is it a smattering of book-learning acquired for the purpose of passing ordination examinations and then left severely alone in the supposed interests of more "practical" concerns. The priest who does not continue his reading and so draw upon the stored-up and ever-increasing riches of theological scholarship is failing in one of the essentials of his craft.

For theology, though it depends upon knowledge, is more than erudition for erudition's sake, more than accumulated information about historical figures and their ideas on theological topics. The priest will study the Bible and the doctrines of the Faith under the impulse of other motives and for other ends. He will remember, first, that theology is the stuff of his preaching, since it gives that ordered, intelligible form to the mysteries of the divine revelation upon which communication with other minds depends. Preaching is, indeed, more than teaching; but if it is not to sink into merely emotional rhetoric it must contain teaching as well as persuasion and appeal. Again, the priest is not only the divinely commissioned minister to other men. Theology is the rational and intelligible pattern of that saving Gospel by which he himself lives his Christian life and from which he derives that body of convictions which control his whole personal outlook on all things in heaven and earth. Most intimately of all, it is the ground of his communion with God. For the God with whom he has to do is not some vaguely conceived supreme being, some hypothetical ground of existence. God for the Christian is the Holy and Undivided Trinity. He is the God who has revealed himself, and whose self-revelation cannot be expressed or proclaimed, whose love cannot be truly known except in terms of Creation, Incarnation, Atonement, Spirit, Church, Baptism, Eucharist, Eternal Life. To pray to that God is to pray theologically. And the converse is also true. The theology is either mere theory, a speculative exercise, or a department of the history of ideas, unless it masters life and brings men to their knees in adoration, thanksgiving, supplication, and penitence.

Study and prayer, then, are bound together by an indivisible link. They are mutually complementary "spiritual exercises", each fertilizing and nourishing the other. The priest's methodical study of the Bible, the creed, and the Liturgy continually renews and deepens the faith from which prayer emerges. His prayer sends him back again to explore those riches of Christ which are inexhaustible. We need to be critical of the too sharp distinction that has sometimes been drawn, in comparatively modern times, between "spiritual reading" and "theological study". The first has been counted a department of prayer, while the second has been excluded. There is, indeed, obvious reason for some kind of distinction. But I wonder what spiritual masters like Origen, St Augustine, and St Benedict would have made of the "either-or" way of dealing with this matter. They would, I suspect, have bidden us not to forget our theology in our spiritual reading, but rather to let theological truth feed and fortify all our prayer. And they would have frowned on any theological study that was not at the same time a communing with him who is the way, the truth, and the life. The study and the prayer that unite in fruitful combination in the *lectio divina* of the monastic tradition can shape an ideal which every priest should make his own as every year, on the anniversary of his ordination, he inwardly renews his vow and rededicates himself to that "diligence" to which he is committed.

The same kind of excessiveness appears in the warnings we sometimes read against mixing up meditation and sermon preparation. Once again the intention seems better than the precept. Obviously the two are not identical. We meditate in order that we may pray to God, not directly in order that we may convert, edify, or exhort other men. But it is difficult to the point of impossibility to cut ourselves in two, or to keep meditation in a watertight compartment. Nor is it good that we should try to do so. For is it really a good way of preparing a sermon to make it an activity in which we are not frequently lifting up the mind to God in conscious and deliberate prayer, all the time submitting ourselves to the godly motives of the Spirit? And, again, are we to suppose that the insights that God has given us in our times of mental prayer are not to inform our preaching? A great phrase of St Thomas Aquinas, *tradere aliis contemplata*, will give us the right answer.

We need not walk with quite such nervously careful steps in our Father's house. Certainly, when a priest sits down in his study to read a commentary or a theological treatise, he will never suppose that he is thereby excused from his daily office or his set times of mental prayer. That would be grievous damage to his spiritual life. But he is also damaging

7

his spiritual life if his office and meditation are not being fertilized and fed by his reading; if St Augustine and Father Benson are never to help him to pray the psalms better; if Westcott and Hoskyns and Lightfoot are never to throw light upon the lections from St John when they come round in his daily office.

3

A learned and wise guide in spiritual things, the late Dom John Chapman, used to say, and say truly, "the more you pray, the better it goes". If that meant the multiplication of offices, longer periods on one's knees in church, the busy parish priest might think it a discouraging aphorism, condemning him to an unprogressive and frustrated prayer life. And he may have read this chapter with the same kind of doubt whether his ceaseless activities for the souls entrusted to him can possibly allow a sufficient margin for that interior life of study and prayer which we have been commending to him. But the saints and spiritual masters have never confined the interior life to set forms of devotion; and they have generally been extremely busy people. What they plead for is "the ascent of the mind to God", the "closer walk" with God. And one way, to say the least of it, in which the priest can put this into practice is by bringing into closer relationship these two activities of prayer and study to which every priest, as such, is bound by his solemn promise and vow at his ordination. Some time he must find. It may be less than he would wish because of the endless pressure of pastoral duties. But fidelity here is more than arithmetic, steady continuance more than mere quantity of time. If he organizes the time he has, letting his reading minister to his prayer and his prayer move him to still deeper study of God's revelation in Christ, he will carry into his "busy-ness" a growing habit of recollection which will spread the atmosphere of prayer over all his comings and goings. The life of prayer is not confined to the cloister, nor is the life of theological study confined to the professor's chamber. Study and prayer are the vital nourishment of the apostolic ministry. Its apostolicity appears when it is "nourished in the words of faith and good doctrine",[1] in "the sacred writings which are able to make thee wise unto salvation through faith which is in Christ Jesus".[2] It appears when we can say with the apostle, "I will pray with the spirit, and I will pray with the understanding also".[3]

[1] 1 Tim. 4. 6.   [2] 2 Tim. 3. 15.   [3] 1 Cor. 14. 15.

9

THE PRIEST TO THE ALTAR

1

Whether he be a profound theologian or not, the priest knows that the crowning privilege of his vocation is the celebration of the Holy Mysteries. That is the lesson of experience, no less than of theology. As the Church knows itself to be what it truly is, the messianic community of the redeemed, when it gathers round the Lord's table; so the priest, when he takes the bread and the cup, gives thanks, breaks the bread, and gives the Body and Blood of Christ to the faithful, knows his priesthood in its central and most fully expressive operation. As Christian and as priest, he finds the Eucharist at the centre of his spiritual life.

This experience derives in large measure from his pastoral relation to the flock of Christ. The celebration of the Eucharist is not a private privilege, confined to a clerical minority and practised for personal edification. It is a liturgical function in and for the Body of Christ, a sacrificial and sacramental ministry, in which the priest acts for and with the people of God in offering the Christian sacrifice and shares with them in the reception of the sacrament. The term "private mass" is ambiguous. As a way of indicating a celebration of the Eucharist at which the priest has only his server to represent the laity it is convenient in practice; but such a celebration is not "private" in the sense of being different in kind from the "public" celebrations at which a general congregation assists. It is the same Eucharist, the same action of Christ in his Body, the Church, whether the worshippers present be many or few. No "private" mass is intended to *exclude* the laity.

Yet the place of the Eucharist in the priest's life is not to be understood simply and solely in terms of his pastoral office. There is an inward as well as an outward reference. His interior life as well as his ministry to his people is conditioned by the Eucharist. This is obviously true in the sense that he, like every devout Christian who values the sacramental life of the Church, finds the Eucharist the focal point in his spiritual exercises. This need not necessarily require him to celebrate every day, but he will do so as frequently as he can, and as he discerns right and good for his spiritual health. It will be part of his rule of life, and an indispensable part, to maintain, with fullest possible measure, his sacramental union with God. But there is another way in which the priest is closely associated with the altar, namely, his specific relation to Christ in his mystical Body.

2

The priest, in virtue of his office, stands at the altar to say the words of Christ and to perform his acts. He is the ministerial agent of the unseen Consecrator. This is his inalienable "liturgy", not better or holier than the "liturgy" of the laity, but different functionally from theirs. It gives the priest his own peculiarly close and intimate part in the offering of the Christian sacrifice, without in any way obscuring or diminishing the "mystical union that is betwixt Christ and his Church" through the sacramental life of the whole Body. Hooker, writing in his majestic prose of "Christ's ambassadors and his labourers", makes special reference to the eucharistic functions of the clergy.[1] "The power of the ministry of God translateth out of darkness into glory, it raiseth men from the earth and bringeth God himself down from heaven, by blessing visible elements it maketh them invisible grace, it giveth daily the Holy Ghost, it hath to dispose of that flesh which was given for the life of the world and that blood which was poured out to redeem souls." This exalted conception of the priestly office is no self-glorification of a sacerdotal caste; it rests upon Christ's commission to his apostles, as the New Testament describes it; and it is adjectival to that substantive priesthood of the Lord himself, from which all ministerial priesthood derives as a delegated and subordinate activity, essentially dependent and secondary.

We may perhaps put it in this way. Christ is not to be identified simply and wholly with his mystical Body. The New Testament, while it speaks of the Church as the Body of Christ, speaks also of Christ as the head of the Body. In Romans and 1 Corinthians the differentiation of Christ as "the head" of "the body" does not appear [2] but in Colossians and Ephesians "the body" is identified with the Church, whereas Christ is the head. The two modes of expression are fused in Ephesians 1. 22, 23, where Christ is "head over all things to the Church, which is his body". The distinction is, as Thornton says, "subsidiary to the main conception, namely, that Christ and his people share one single life together after a manner which can be fully symbolized by the idea of a single human organism".[3] But it is a real dis-

---

[1] *Ecclesiastical Polity*, V, 77.

[2] See Thornton, *The Common Life in the Body of Christ*, pp. 46f.

[3] Ibid., p. 48.

tinction, and a necessary one for the theological understanding of Christ's relation to his Church and to the ministry.

In the life of the Church the mystery of Christ's High Priesthood manifests itself in two modes, which are analogous to the Christ-Body and the Church-Head imagery. There is, on the one hand, the corporate, baptismal priesthood of the whole Church, stated in 1 Peter 2. 5, 9; Rev. 1. 6. Here, the priesthood of Christ is representatively active in the sacrificial living of the members of his mystical Body, that "worship" of which St Paul writes in Romans 12. The corporate life of the baptized is meant to be sacrificial and priestly, an oblation of loving obedience, the Christ-life realized in the members of Christ. It is the life of the "New Israel", of the "adopted sons", of the "branches" of the Vine. But Christ, who brought to birth from the Old Israel the messianic community of the New Covenant, also created the apostolate, and commissioned his apostolic ministers to perform in his name certain specific functions within, and for the perpetuation of, that community. He bade them "feed my sheep", "preach", "baptize", "do this in remembrance of me". Here is the action of the head of the Body.

The works of Christ go on: Pentecost, the Church, the Sacraments, the proclamation of the Gospel are as much his work as the Galilean ministry, the passion and the death, the rising on the third day. And the continuing apostolate still shares his work, as he commissioned it to do in the days of his flesh.[1]

The apostolate is an essential datum of the New Testament. That is beyond question, whether we look at the gospels, or the Acts, or the Pauline epistles. We might indeed have expected it from the whole sacred history

[1] Mark 3. 14, 15; 4. 10, 11.

of Israel that lies behind the Gospel. For in that Old Testament background we have such things as Moses' appointment of leaders of the tribes (Num. 1. 17) and judges (Ex. 18. 25). We have also the twelve patriarchs; and the number "twelve" cannot but be more than accidental, when Jesus called men to be the patriarchs of the New Israel. But we are not left with types and their possible or probable fulfilments. The New Testament states explicitly that the apostles are directly appointed to act as Christ's representatives: they are sent by him to be fishers of men, to be the stewards of the Lord's household, princes enthroned in the Messiah's kingdom, shepherds of the flock.[1] In Matthew 10 we read how they are to continue and extend the Lord's work as his agents and representatives. In Matthew 28. 19 the proclamation of the Gospel to all nations is added to the pastoral oversight of the flock.

The epistles and Acts show how apostleship remained after Pentecost, in undisputed leadership and authority: undisputed because Christ had "set apostles first" in the Church. And when we pass from the New Testament to the early Fathers, to Clement, Ignatius, Irenaeus, it is obvious that Christianity meant to them "a complex of belief and practice which in the final resort went back to Christ himself", but for which "the immediately accessible authorities" were the prophets of Israel and the apostles who had worked with Christ and whom he had commissioned.[2] It is the *apostolic* tradition that lies behind the Christian preaching and teaching, the New Testament Canon and the creeds, the eucharistic worship, and the threefold ministry of bishops, presbyters, and deacons.

---

[1] Mark 1. 17; Luke 12. 42; 12. 29, 30; John 21. 15–17.
[2] Cf. J. N. D. Kelly, *Early Christian Doctrines*, p. 31.

It is sometimes denied that apostleship remains in the Church. It is alleged that it ceased with the original eye-witnesses. But this negative fails to take account of all the evidence.

It is certainly true that some of the features of the original group of apostles—i.e. the twelve reconstructed by the addition of Matthias—are not transmissible. Obviously, only the eleven were chosen by the Lord in the days of his flesh. And the inalienable privilege of the eleven, of St Matthias and of St Paul, was to be eyewitnesses of the risen Christ, with a certain, not unimportant, difference in the case of St Paul. But the New Testament evidence does not by any manner of means say that apostleship cannot exist except in those who had been companions of the Lord and eyewitnesses. The apostle had other essential functions; and those functions are in their very nature bound up with the continuing existence of the Church. If the Church remains, they remain.

The Swedish scholar, Professor H. Riesenfeld,[1] has drawn attention to four New Testament images which show one common structure in the Church, and the apostolic office as an integral part of that structure. Christ is the master of the household (Matt. 10. 25) and the Church is a household or family, in which the apostles are stewards (Luke 12. 42) entrusted with keys of stewardship (Matt. 16. 19). Again, Christ is the head cornerstone (Mark 12. 10; Eph. 2. 20–2), and the Church is a temple of living stones (1 Pet. 2. 5) with the apostles and prophets lesser foundation stones (Eph. 2. 20) or, alternatively, master-builders (1 Cor. 3. 9). Thirdly, Christ is the bridegroom and the Church the bride (Eph. 5. 25–32; cf. Matt. 22. 2; 25. 1).

[1] See his paper, *Ministry in the New Testament*, in the volume entitled *The Root of the Vine*.

The apostle's work is to bring the bride to the bridegroom (2 Cor. 11. 2). Fourthly, Christ is the shepherd (John 10. 11–16; 1 Pet. 5. 4) and the Church the flock. The apostles are under-shepherds charged to feed the sheep (John 21. 15–17).

If we are to give due weight to all this, it seems inevitable to infer that functions assigned to the apostles are permanently necessary in the Church, and that in this sense the ministry is correctly described as apostolic. And, since the method employed by the Lord and consistently followed by the early Church was the method of commission by those already entrusted with these functions, the principle of apostolic succession seems reasonably secure.

The Lord, then, chose, and still chooses, men to be his spokesmen and representatives, to share the work of the head under his authority and for the Gospel's sake. And nowhere do these men realize how high a dignity and how weighty an office and charge are entrusted to them than when they stand at the altar to say the words and do the acts of Christ in the holy mysteries of the eucharistic sacrifice. For the priest has this dual relationship to Christ: first, as a member of his mystical Body, like every other faithful Christian, and then as Christ's apostolic delegate, exercising a ministry of Christ which finds its sharpest and clearest focus in the celebration of the Eucharist. Therein lies the special privilege, very high and very humbling, of his office. The bond that binds the priest to the altar and makes the Eucharist the centre of his prayer life is a profoundly theological apprehension of Christ, an imperative that issues from the very heart of the Gospel of redemption. It is not only pastoral zeal that makes the priest want to celebrate frequently; nor is the priest at fault when he feels that to celebrate himself and to receive communion from the hands of another priest are not quite the same thing. His life and vocation as a priest cry out for his own "liturgy". Nothing can take its place. Infirmity or other untoward circumstances may prevent him from celebrating as they may rob him of the exercise of other functions of his priesthood. But as long as he can go to the altar of God, there he will want to stand.

3

There is yet another way in which the Eucharist touches his priesthood closely, indeed at the deepest levels of his dedication.

As there is, in the full sense, only one teacher and rabbi, one pastor, evangelist, and prophet—the Lord himself—so there is only one priest. When these terms are applied to the Christian bishop and presbyter, they apply only in a secondary, ministerial, sense. The human agents do not act in their own name, but in the name of their principal. Yet that does not mean that their ministry is merely that of living tools or animated puppets in Christ's hands. It is a ministry on the personal, not the mechanical, level. Personality operates through conscious wills and purposeful self-identification with souls deliberately chosen and adopted. Hence it is an intimate union of will, a purposeful dedication of the self, that Christ desires from those who speak his words and perform his acts for the people of God. It follows that the eucharistic life of the human priest goes far deeper than the careful and dutiful performance of ceremonial and ritual functions. It is nothing less than an entering into the mystery of Christ as victim as well as priest—an interior oblation of the self and an imparted share in the sacrificial obedience of the son to his Father.

The author of the Epistle to the Hebrews does not hesitate to say that Christ "having been heard for his godly fear, though he was a son, yet learned obedience by the things which he suffered".[1] If that priesthood "after the order of Melchisedek", which is Christ's, is the only source of true priesthood, then the ministerial priesthood of men must seek to present the authentic stamp of him who could be our High Priest because he was "holy, guileless, undefiled" and "offered himself without blemish unto God'. Christ, indeed, has "offered one sacrifice for sins for ever" and the victimhood of his human priests can add nothing to the saving merits of the one mediator. Yet Christ the victim must appear in the human priest just as really as Christ the pastor and Christ the teacher. If it were not so, the ministry would fail to be representative at the deeper levels, the level of personal dedication; for it would not be a ministry of persons, of dedicated wills capable, by God's grace, of voluntary, loving obedience.

There is no limit to what this demands of the priest in the way of self-surrender and a passionate longing for God. Sacrificial office and functions must march with sacrificial living. There is a phrase that has often been used of the priest: *alter Christus*. It is a dangerous phrase, easily perverted. It may make a sensitive mind shiver with alarm at what might seem presumptuous rhetoric. Yet it is capable of expressing a most necessary truth about the relation of the human priest to the great High Priest: the priest *of* Christ must be the priest *in* Christ. If it is held in the mind as a warning and a challenge, summoning to a deeper penitence, a more confident faith, and a more sacrificial love, it will serve.

If the ritual oblation which the priest makes at the altar

[1] Heb. 5. 7, 8.

thus enters deeply into the personal oblation of himself, soul and body, as a living sacrifice, his whole life becomes eucharistic, a *sacrificium laudis*. What Dom Gregory Dix taught us to call the "Shape of the Liturgy" will mould his character, discipline his will, and govern his actions. The four "moments" of the Liturgy are offertory, thanksgiving, fraction, and communion; and those can be seen as the essence of the priest's spiritual life. He offers his work, his ministry, his people, himself on the altar of God. He calls down the power of God upon them that they may be all transmuted by being caught up into union with Christ, who is both our High Priest and the Lamb of God. He breaks the Lord's Body in pieces, and as he does so he is mindful of how he is to make a costly, sacrificial expenditure of himself, his time, his strength, and his energy, for there are many whom he is to serve; and he is not his own, he is a minister. But the crown of the sacrificial action is communion, that fellowship with God through the Holy Spirit in the Body of Christ which is the foretaste of eternity and the earnest of our inheritance. The whole is sacrifice—the "making-sacred" not merely of what man has but of what man is, through the merits and mediation of the Son of Man.

Thus it is that in the Eucharist which he offers week by week or day by day the priest continually learns afresh what his priesthood truly is. He learns it and at the same time he gains power to live it. Above all he will seek to learn not only to do but also to suffer with patience and charity and to receive the power to make these graces effective in his daily work of ministry. For as at the heart of the Eucharist there is the passion and cross of Christ, so in the eucharistic life of the priest there must be the mark of the cross. The life of the priest to-day is hard. It has many trials, both external and internal. Economic stress is all too familiar; and it is accompanied by the many heartaches and disappointments of the pastoral ministry. The perils of resentment, despondency, and even despair are about the priest's path, and he knows it. But if he enters, with patience, faith, and humility, into the mystery of the eucharistic sacrifice, he will be fortified against these things. He will come to know that, as he is a sharer in Christ's priesthood, suffering is bound to enter into his life. And, because he is a priest, he would not have it otherwise.

10

THE WORK OF GOD

1

The work of God, *opus Dei*, was the name given by St Benedict to the divine office, that daily course of ordered worship which was to be the principal and most jealously guarded duty of his monks. It is to the monks that the Church owes the office, for it was they who first gave it systematic shape. Not that the worship of God by the recitation of psalms, the reading of the Scriptures, and the singing of hymns was in itself a monastic novelty. It was older than monasticism, being part of our heritage from Judaism. It appears in the primitive synaxis (the "ante-communion" service) and in the private devotions of devout Christians. But the addition of the divine office, as common liturgical prayer, to the central Christian worship of the Eucharist, and what immediately introduced the Eucharist, came as a borrowing by the secular clergy from the monasteries. The immense value of the office was thus first tested and established in the spiritual life of the "athletes of God". Then it came to be known over a much wider field, when it was transplanted into popular worship and became part of the regular liturgical prayer of the clergy and the devout laity.

The fully developed liturgical office, spread over the day at intervals from midnight to sunset, from the night office to Compline, is too long and too elaborate for general use by lay Christians, and it has of necessity been confined in its fullness to the monasteries and later to the secular clergy. Yet in the early centuries of the Church's life this kind of prayer, based on the Psalter and other Scriptures, was far from being wholly restricted to monks and clerics, as appears from such documents as the *Peregrinatio Etheriae* (about A.D. 385). A morning and an evening office were the best attended, but some lay people went to other offices. In the Middle Ages, too, Mattins (sung before Mass) and Evensong were attended by lay people on Sundays and festivals. But from the twelfth century it had become generally accepted that the offices were mainly a matter for the clergy. In the simplified and much reduced form of the office found in the Book of Common Prayer a notable attempt was made to go back to the principle that the office belongs to the whole Christian body, clerics and laity alike. It has had no small measure of success. The daily Evensong which in cathedrals and many parish churches all over England gathers a few of the faithful round their priests for "the work of God" is a precious element in the spiritual life of the Church of England. Nevertheless, the daily office remains, and in the circumstances of modern life is likely to remain, largely the responsibility of the clergy. This, indeed, the Book of Common Prayer seems to expect. For it lays a strict injunction upon priests and deacons to say the daily office, but it recognizes that invitation, not injunction, is all that can be addressed to the laity.

2

Ancient tradition, then, as well as the explicit statement of the Book of Common Prayer, gives to the priest as a

primary duty the daily recitation of the office. The obligation is one for which he can be grateful, since the office
enters into his spiritual life as an element second only to the
Eucharist in its importance and its formative influence.
Even if he does not celebrate the Holy Mysteries every day,
yet in the office he takes his place in the Church's unceasing
offering of divine worship and day by day shares in "the
work of God". The more he understands his priesthood
and the greater the value he attaches to it, the more will he
cherish the duty and privilege of this liturgical prayer. Nor
is it enough to think of the office in terms of duty and privilege. The faithful use of it is of untold value for his own
spiritual growth and maturity.

There are many reasons why this should be so. First
among such reasons is that the daily office is supremely the
priest's school of prayer. Christian prayer is determined by
the biblical revelation of God, and the office is built mainly
of biblical material. So the office disciplines and controls
the innate prayer-impulse by subjecting it to the divine
revelation. By it prayer is firmly linked with the redemptive
purpose of God through Israel and through Christ and his
Church. The heart of the office is the recitation of the
Psalter in course. At first sight this may look like a reversion
to pre-Christian modes of devotion. Why, it may be asked,
these Jewish psalms, and why has the Church not composed
her own Psalter? It is a worthwhile question, for the answer
takes us to the foundations of the Gospel, to the fulfilment
of the hope of Israel in Christ.

The whole of the old covenant—its history, religious
institutions, and ideas—is preparatory and prophetic. The
aspirations of the psalmists and prophets of Israel do not
hang in the air; they are fulfilled in Christ. Hence the
Psalter, the religious heart of the Old Testament, comes to
8

its proper use only as its language is understood in its Christian reference. The psalms become the Church's prayer with far greater fullness of meaning than they ever had as the prayer of the synagogue. This content of meaning, it may be said, is imposed upon the words. So it is, but it is imposed by the facts, if the Christian estimate of Jesus is accepted as the truth, and St Luke's account of the instruction given by the risen Christ to the disciples (Luke 24. 44–7) is substantially correct. The royal psalms, the judgement psalms, and the priestly psalms come into their own, when in Christian prayer they are referred to Christ and God's purpose in Christ. They are hymns of Christ. Another group, the gradual psalms, and the historical psalms of the Exodus, the exile, and the return, may be called the hymns of the Church. And in the great psalms sometimes called nature psalms or cosmic psalms creation and redemption are united as acts of the one God who by his divine Word is the maker and redeemer of all things.

So it is not as isolated specimens of noble religious poetry that the priest recites the psalms. Nor does he regard them only as expressions of the manifold ways in which the individual, in the privacy of his own personal life and devotion, can open his heart to the ever-present God. This or that psalm will, indeed, provide the incomparable vehicle for such intimate communion, as *solus cum solo* the individual soul lays its concerns before God. But the psalms have another meaning and their daily recitation rests on something more than their subjective value for private devotion.

The psalms are the prayer of Christ and his mystical Body. St Augustine, in his great work on the psalms, at a number of points presses home this essential character of the psalms in the devotional life of the Church. Thus, commenting on Psalm 57 (Vulgate 56), he writes:

The whole Christ is Head and Body—the Head our Saviour, who suffered, rose again, and is seated at the right hand of the Father; the Body His Church, not this Church or that Church, but the Church spread throughout the world; nor, again, merely the Church that now exists among men at present alive, but including the men that have been before us, and those that shall come after us even to the end of the world—the whole Church, I say, consisting of all the faithful, for all the faithful are members of Christ. The Head of this Church is set in heaven, governing His Body, screened off from view, but united in charity. Therefore in all the psalms let us hear at once the cries of the Head and the cries of the Body.

He makes the same point in expounding Psalm 38 (Vulgate 37):

When Christ speaks, sometimes He speaks in the person of the Head alone, which is our Saviour Himself, born of the Virgin Mary; sometimes in the person of His Body, which is the Holy Church diffused throughout the world.

This principle of interpretation is firmly grounded in the unity of the biblical revelation, as St Augustine says in his exposition of Psalm 114 (Vulgate 113):

If we retain with a firm heart the grace of God given us, we are Israel, the seed of Abraham, as the apostle says: ye are the seed of Abraham. Let no Christian then consider himself a stranger to the name of Israel. All those things that were done then by way of figure are now accomplished in our salvation.

There are other weighty reasons for the central place of the psalms in the daily offices of the Church. The psalms come to us hallowed by Jesus Christ himself, for they were his prayer in his life on earth. They supply the atmosphere of prayer in which the New Testament was written. They have been the prayer of the martyrs and all the saints; and, no less, they have nourished the devotion of the ordinary, wayfaring Christian throughout the centuries. Schooled in the psalms, the priest indeed enters upon a great heritage and can build his spiritual life securely on the foundation of the apostles and prophets, Jesus Christ himself being the chief cornerstone.

Yet, though tradition confers upon the psalms such high dignity and authority, it is not only upon tradition that their appeal rests. The psalms have a remarkable adaptability. For they lend themselves equally well to the objective prayer of the Church's Liturgy and to the intimate private prayer of the individual. In their range and variety of mood there is something for every constituent element in the spiritual life of man. There are psalms that soar up to God in a surge of adoring faith, others that mirror an almost despairing distress and darkness of soul. Life is never sentimentalized—the bitter and the sweet, the rough and the smooth are presented with a realism that does not flinch but faces all the facts; and it is no small proof of the Psalter's undying vitality and relevance that those who have used it every day for many years are those who still find in it an unfailing source of spiritual nourishment.

The psalms, then, with their accompanying "lections", prayers and hymns, are the staple food of the priest's spiritual life. Encircling the central act of the Eucharist, and drawing their full and proper meaning from that to which the Eucharist bears its unique testimony, namely the living Lord of the Church, the psalms hold the priest close to the Bible, and to the saving Gospel of which he is the minister. All other devotional aids and practices are subordinate to this complex of the Eucharist and the divine office, for all of them serve only to send him back to the Incarnate Word, whose atoning sacrifice he presents in the Eucharist and whose saving Gospel he is ever learning, and relearning, to know from the Scriptures.

3

The liturgical use of the psalms in Christian worship is no piece of unreasoning conservatism. It rests on a principle. It depends upon their application to Christ and his Church, and this, as we have seen, is the tradition of the Church from the age of the Fathers. How this application may be made can be shown by an example.

One of the unvarying psalms of Compline, Psalm 91, will serve admirably, all the more so because it is as familiar as any part of Scripture to thousands of priests who recite it every day of their lives and know it by heart. This psalm, originally, may have had its roots in primitive levels of religious emotion. It would be easy to see in it a kind of protective charm against the perils, natural and preternatural, of a journey through the desert. The traveller seems to see himself in danger. The danger is of various kinds; raiding bedouin, wild beasts, poisonous serpents threaten his safety. And, more dreadful still, there are the demons that haunt desert places; for that is the probable meaning of verse 6, where the Septuagint text, with its "demon of the noonday", comes closer to the original sense than the familiar Prayer Book rendering, "the sickness that destroyeth in the noonday". Against all this the primitive traveller seeks divine protection.

Taken then at its face value, the psalm does not seem to be of more than antiquarian interest; it is a bit of evidence for the student of primitive religious ideas rather than a Christian prayer. And we need not suppose that it came to be included in the Jewish Canon without some modification of its meaning, some translation of its content with the help of symbolic interpretation, so that it could be given a wider, more general reference than it originally had. But whatever may have been the pre-Christian literary history of this poem—and that for lack of evidence must remain problematical—its use in Christian prayer is not determined by that history.

For the praying Church this psalm becomes a noble affirmation that the Church's security, in all the hazards of her pilgrimage, is her faith in God and his Christ. Day by day in her evening prayers she reminds herself of the rock which is Christ, the rock of impregnable truth. She sees in the psalmist's imagery the Christian's temptations and the spiritual resources that he has at his disposal. There are the snares of spiritual wickedness, the corrupting poisons of worldiness, the fears and anxieties and despondences that lurk in the shadowy corners of the soul. There is the sudden arrow-shot of unexpected temptation, hitting the pilgrim Christian when he is off his guard. There are the unseen spiritual enemies, which in dark hours seek to betray him into pride and jealousy, resentment, self-pity, and all the manifold forms of self-love. And there is that "noonday demon", which for some monastic writers has meant the sin of *accidie*, but which may symbolize equally well every kind of mortal sin, that sin which is committed in the full light, deliberately and knowingly, the most perilous sin of all.

Against all this there is the armour of faith, that panoply of God of which the apostle writes in Ephesians 6. "Thou shalt not be afraid" rings with all the overtones of Christ's reassuring words in the gospels. Whatever be the destructive powers of evil and the weakness of man the sinner, there is in the crucified and risen Christ full protection and the pledge of victory.

"Because he hath set his love upon me", "because he

hath known my name". So the psalm brings the Christian
back to the revealing of the name of God as the final
assurance. In Christ he finds the revelation of a divine
concern and a divine purpose for man, a purpose of love
backed by invincible power. The outcome of that loving
purpose is nothing less than eternal life, the life of the
adopted sons of God.

So seen, the psalm is a kind of daily thanksgiving in the
form of a devotional commentary on the Christian Faith.
The Most High, the Almighty—so the psalm (like the creed)
begins with God the Father Almighty. Thus we are led to
thankful recognition of man's deliverance by him who for
us men and for our salvation came down from heaven, and
so to the house of defence set very high, that Holy Church
which is the Body of Christ and the ark of salvation. The
Christian, sharing the resurrection life of Christ, is to share
its victory over evil through the forgiveness of sins and the
new life conferred in baptism and nourished by the
Eucharist. And the conclusion is "with long life will I
satisfy him": that abiding life which is eternal and is
crowned by the beatific vision—"I will show him my
salvation".

So the great themes unroll themselves. "Reading between
the lines"? Yes, of course. But not in any arbitrary or
merely fanciful way, if we accept the fundamental Christian
conviction that the revelation of God through Israel and
Jesus Christ is a unity in multiplicity; if with the author of
the Epistle to the Hebrews we hold that the one God, who
spoke to the fathers in the prophets "by divers portions and
in divers manners", "hath at the end of their days spoken
unto us in his Son, whom he appointed heir of all things".
It is only from the vantage ground of the Christian Faith
that we can find in the psalms prophetic language that

expresses, and expresses with such singular and arresting fitness, the glory that was to be revealed; that glory to which the Old Testament prophets, psalmists, priests, and sages dimly and uncomprehendingly pointed, but pointed better than they knew.

11

BEHIND THE SHUT DOOR

Christian prayer is the prayer of those who, in St Paul's phrase, are "in Christ" and also are "led by the Spirit of God". Hence it is essentially the prayer of the Church, which is the Body of Christ and the temple of the Spirit. It is participation in the prayer of Christ and his members, of the *totus Christus*, an entering into the self-oblation of Christ, a co-operation with the Spirit who himself "maketh intercession for us". The individual Christian, certainly, does not lose his personal distinctiveness or swoon, as in some kind of anaesthetic mist, when he betakes himself to prayer. But, remaining an individual person, he does at the same time pray as a member of the mystical Body, sharing the larger prayer life of the Church, praying in the Spirit. Primarily he does this by taking his own part in the Liturgy, the centre of the Church's life as it faces God.

The central place of the Liturgy has been rediscovered, or at least freshly appreciated, in our own day. That has been undoubted gain. Yet, remembering the unfortunate human tendency to be dazzled by a new enthusiasm, we have to be on our guard. A reaction against the individualism and emotionalism of much post-Renaissance piety, both catholic and protestant, was eminently desirable. It must not, however, be allowed to reach the point of suggesting that liturgical prayer and private devotional exercises in the inner chamber are mutually exclusive, or in some sort of opposition. Nothing could be further from the truth. Both for himself and for the people to whom he ministers the priest has to realize that it is the Liturgy itself which makes private interior prayer an absolute necessity in the Christian life.

To reach that conclusion we need only to call to mind some fundamental principles of Christian prayer.

1

Prayer, in the light of the biblical revelation, is not an occasional appeal to a higher power for help when we can do nothing more for ourselves and have to fall back on divine aid.[1] It is a function of our sonship. As "adopted sons", in St Paul's phrase, we have fellowship with the Father in the daily intercourse of the household of God, sharing all our activities with him and directing all to the one purpose of doing his will in filial, loving obedience. Prayer in all its aspects—as adoration, thanksgiving, petition, intercession, penitence—is the inevitable corollary of this relationship, its direct, personal realization in practice. Now the biblical account of this relationship contains two co-ordinate emphases. First, there is the emphasis on the people of God, to whom are given the promises. We are members one of another, and the redeemed *community*. We are linked in a corporate life that determines the character of prayer as something shared, not merely the secret communion of the isolated individual with his God. But the Bible no more deals with men as mere components of a social structure than it treats them as bare individuals. The second emphasis, clearly visible throughout, is on the individual person as a morally responsible being, dear to

[1] Cf. A. A. Lilley, *Prayer in Christian Theology.*

God, unique in his or her personal selfhood. To put it in more abstract terms, human nature, as God created it, has two focuses: man is at once a social being and a spiritual person. In the language of simple Christian piety, "Christ died for mankind and Christ died for me".[1]

Christian prayer mirrors these facts. It holds together liturgical prayer and private prayer as complementaries. Liturgy is corporate prayer, using ordered forms and patterns so that all may know what is being done and may join in a common action. It is mainly objective, presenting the mysteries of redemption to the worshipping congregation as the acts of God that call forth the response of Christians in faith and love and worship. Liturgy, too, being corporate is necessarily generalized in its content. In all these respects, as corporate, objective, and general, it demands its complement, the personal appropriation by the individual soul of what the liturgical forms present, and the particular application of divine truth and divine grace to the individual's own needs, purposes, hopes, fears, desires. In part this can be done during the course of the liturgical action, and indeed must be done, in some measure, if the Liturgy is not to be reduced to an empty form. But, because the Liturgy is a comparatively rapid action, with frequent transitions and the compression of great matters, vital to the Christian life, in short, general phrases, there is a pressing need for more time, for unfettered dwelling upon the material presented, for a large liberty to make an intimate, personal use of what the Liturgy and the Bible have to say. The individual Christian must learn to speak about all this material to the Father intimately and at leisure, and to

[1] Cf. P. Teilhard de Chardin, *Le Milieu Divin*, pp. 31 f. "The masters of the spiritual life incessantly repeat that God wants only souls. . . . In each soul God loves and partly saves the whole world which that soul sums up in an incommunicable and particular way."

bring into this colloquy the manifold details of his own life and work. And he must also learn to listen. "Hear, Lord, for thy servant speaketh" is not a sufficient rubric for private prayer. We have to enter the inner chamber to hear the Word of God in quietness rather than to make its walls ring with our clamour.

So the priest will remember that, unless he sets himself thus to "read, mark, learn and inwardly digest" the inexhaustible riches of Christ, there can be no progress in the life of prayer, no chance of finding prayer a living and growing experience, and an activity ever richer and more engrossing as he perseveres in it. And this is the sufficient ground for that practice of "mental prayer" which has played so vital a part in Christian spirituality. It is not too much to say that the fruitfulness of the priest's liturgical life, of sacramental communion, and of all vocal prayer, liturgical and private, depends very largely upon mental prayer, in which an intimate fellowship with God in the exercise of our sonship is thrown open to us. As Cardinal Manning once wrote, "this realization of unseen and heavenly things is better than all external rules to guard and strengthen a priest".[1]

2

Does that mean that we set an impossible standard, by shutting the gate into the priesthood against all but a few "mystics"? Not at all. Three things often confused should be carefully distinguished. An interest in the study of mysticism is one thing. An aptitude for mystical experience in prayer is another. But the spiritual life can flourish and bear good fruit with or without the aid of either or both of

[1] *Eternal Priesthood*, p. 99.

these things. The *tertium quid* is the practice of mental prayer, whether in the form of discursive meditation on points of devotional Bible reading or of contemplative quiet. This is for all. It is a matter of general concern to the Christian as such, and *a fortiori* to the Christian priest, however limited may be his knowledge of the history of mysticism or his experience of advanced states of mystical prayer. The elaboration of ascetic and mystical theology through the centuries has produced a vast literature. It has piled up a wealth of information about the soul's adventure in prayer. This mass of psychological description and analysis can be a fascinating study, but for many priests it is somewhat daunting and they are disposed to leave it aside as a subject for specialists rather than for the working pastors of the flock. Doubtless, a real mastery of ascetical and mystical theology does make demands for which many a parish priest has neither the time, nor, it may be, the aptitude. So, too, we ought not to expect of every priest personal experience of the higher flights of mystical prayer, since this is in no way indispensable either for a holy life or for complete devotion to the demands of his calling. But this does not mean that mental prayer itself is a specialist activity or that any priest can afford to dispense with it. It is necessary to realize that mental prayer in some form is vital for the priest's spiritual life. It is equally necessary to grasp the fact that, in substance, mental prayer is no esoteric mystery for an *élite*, but is a way of prayer that is open to all.

For what, in fact, do we mean, or what ought we to mean, by mental prayer? In essence it is a very simple matter, something that praying Christians of all kinds have always practised in one form or another. Just because it has been used so much, it has been studied and written about in innumerable books, wherein are described the many different methods employed by praying people. Some of these methods are more complicated than others, and they have been made to appear more complicated than they really are by the rules and technicalities introduced by those who write about them. Yet elaborate and complicated procedures are not inherent in mental prayer. For mental prayer is as necessary for beginners and for the wayfaring Christian as for those who are advanced in the spiritual life. It is not a hard piece of brain work. No university education is required for proficiency in it. Just because it is the most intimate kind of prayer, it is that in which the individual must have the greatest freedom and ease, and where the necessary intellectual operations are of the most elementary kind. The difficulties that do occur are spiritual, not intellectual; they spring from the imperfection of our faith and perseverance, not from undue demands upon brain power.

All the various methods described by spiritual writers are adaptations, to suit various types of mind and temperament, of the fundamental activity of religion; that is to say, communion with God in deliberate, willed attentiveness to himself for his own sake and in the light of his self-revealing of himself in creation, redemption, and the mission of the Spirit. The method can be simply expressed as ways of making ourselves ready to listen to God. But the metaphor of listening must not be misunderstood. It must not be taken to mean that mental prayer is an ecstatic state in which we hear voices and go into trances and see visions. These psychological phenomena do occur, but they are peripheral and occasional experiences that in no way belong to the essence of prayer; and, generally speaking, they are not to be sought after or expected. The normal way of listening to God is a highway for every man to walk in, not a search for exotic experiences. When God speaks to man, he speaks through Christ, who is the Word of God. Principally, though not exclusively (since God is not bound by his own revelation), he speaks through the life and teaching of the Incarnate Word, made known to us by the Bible and the Church. Our listening to God is thus our receptivity to the Gospel. It operates by the direction of thought and will towards the understanding of the mysteries of the Faith, in order that life may be progressively mastered by them and oriented more successfully Godwards. Methods of doing this are many and various, but the aim is one and the same. The aim is common to the simplest kind of devotional Bible reading, such as devout evangelical Christians have practised for centuries, to the more formally organized three-point meditation or the prayer of simple regard, and to the advanced states of mystical prayer known to a St Teresa or a St John of the Cross. The most practically minded and extroverted Christian, busy with many things, can, if he will, take a passage from the gospels—it may be a sentence or even a single word; he can dwell upon it, seek its meaning and application to himself, and then turn it into material for speaking to God and listening attentively to what God is saying to him. In doing that, he is doing in substance the very thing that all the technical terms—discursive meditation, affective prayer, acquired contemplation, prayer of quiet and simple regard—are describing with fuller analytical precision.

These technical distinctions are valuable, and indispensable as guides to the great variety and the wide freedom of this most intimate and personal approach to God. But they are not themselves more than descriptive labels. The masters of prayer unite in warning against any dependence on a particular technique. Their positive emphasis is on such things as devout preparation for prayer, attention to the divine revelation in a docile and practical spirit, the pre-eminence of the gospels as material, the results of prayer in the transformation of life, the importance of using what we find profitable rather than the carrying-out of any set plan, the supreme need of following the godly motions of the Holy Spirit. Methods, that is to say, are useful in so far as they lead to communion with God and conversion of life.

3

Father Benson of Cowley, whose heroic sanctity and mastery of the spiritual life are beyond dispute, has given valuable advice on mental prayer in the introduction to his book of meditations, *Benedictus Dominus*. In the course of it he says these wise words:

By the Sacraments God takes hold of us and works invisibly in us. By meditation we take hold upon His invisible Presence, feed upon Him in our souls, receive the illumination of His Holy Spirit, grow in grace and become perfectly united to Him. By it we exercise Faith, which is the substance of things hoped for, the evidence of things not seen.

And again:

We do not see the things of the world unless we choose to gaze upon them. . . . For want of meditation, therefore, prayer is often ineffectual, sacraments are profitless, the reading of Holy Scripture uninstructive, the knowledge of the true faith void of unction.

No one needs to take these words to heart more than the ministers of the Word and Sacraments. For just because they are occupied all day every day with holy things, they have to be constantly watchful lest they fall into a kind of professional hardness in their attitude to them. No priest worthy of the name could ever regard the grace of God as a mere commodity which he was paid to deal in during business hours. But there is a more subtle danger—that of an unwittingly acquired insensitiveness, which makes the ministry of the Word and Sacraments at best a round of duties to be performed in an honest and businesslike way, and at worst a toilsome routine of parochial chores. It is to be feared that sometimes those clerical mannerisms which the laity deplore—the parsonical voice, the breezy, hearty manner, the ostentatious mouthing of the Liturgy for the sake of effect—are more than failures in technique; that they are, in fact, unconscious compensations for spiritual malnutrition, the starving of the interior life. Be that as it may, we can be reasonably sure that no structure of religious institutions and external practices is ever safe in the hands of men, unless the inward vision is kept clear and bright, and that even the Christian Eucharist and the preaching of the Christian Gospel are not exempt from the operation of this general principle. It is by some method of mental prayer, faithfully and diligently pursued, that the priest can keep the inner vision clear and can strengthen his personal apprehension of those exalted mysteries which are entrusted to his charge for the edifying of the people of God and the salvation of souls.

12

PROGRESS IN PRAYER

We have outlined the threefold pattern of the priest's prayers. This pattern of Eucharist, office, and meditation is no arbitrary scheme contrived for the satisfaction of a private or cloistered piety. Still less is it some "high church" fad. It proceeds straight from the biblical revelation and the teaching of the New Testament. It is certainly catholic; it is as certainly evangelical. It belongs to the Christian centuries and has stamped the prayers of the saints. It is enjoined upon the priests of the Church of England by that Prayer Book which, when all its deficiencies are admitted, remains the authoritative manual of *Ecclesia Anglicana*.

But does it work? The question is not an improper one. A traditional scheme of devotion is neither to be rejected nor to be accepted simply because it is traditional. We may rightly ask whether it ministers of real progress in the spiritual life, for such progress is the best sign of health and reality. What does experience show to be the fruits of this combination of liturgical and mental prayer, when it is practised with perseverance and faith?

1

The first fruit is a deeper penetration into the marvellous interior life of the mystical Body of Christ. That interior life expresses itself primarily in the ceaseless liturgical prayer of the Church. In its yearly rhythm the Liturgy not only unfolds the historical content of the biblical revelation. It does much more. It makes the saving events a contemporary reality. As it catches us up into their abiding life, the Liturgy is no mere commemorative pageant of ancient history but a dynamic action. Thereby the worshipping Church enters into the vital experience of the Christ of Bethlehem and Galilee, the Christ of the upper room, the cross, and the empty tomb, the Christ of the heavenly session and the mission of the Holy Ghost. No longer do we know Christ only "after the flesh", as a gracious figure in a story of long ago, we meet him as the living Lord who was and is and is to come. Supremely is this true in the worship of the Eucharist, that action which is the whole Gospel in effective impact and realization. For the Liturgy reveals to us what the essence of Christianity really is. That essence is not directly accessible to us in a metaphysical system or in an ethical ideal. The Lord came not simply to acquaint us with certain truths about God, the world, and ourselves, though he has in fact revealed more of that truth than any sage or moralist. He came to transform us and the world by a divine action which no created intelligence could ever have foreseen or even conceived. And the way of that transformation is the way of worship: the worship by which the redeemed community is brought under the rule of God.

As the priest, the guardian of the Church's worship, carries out his liturgical duties day by day, he is well aware that he needs constant vigilance against the perils of a merely routine and external recitation of the liturgical forms. His examination of conscience will never be complete without scrutiny of his conduct in that regard. Though he will avoid scrupulosity over the involuntary distractions to which human frailty is always prone, he will not be too easy in excusing himself. Yet his very penitence will be a powerful aid in bringing him to a progressive appreciation of the amazing privilege of liturgical prayer. Love and awe grow as insight deepens. The faithful priest knows that the prayers and lections grow upon him. They meant much to him when at his theological college he first began to recite the daily office. Now after many years they are charged with far greater illumination and power. And they carry the promise of richer blessings still to come.

No less marked is the progress that comes with the faithful practice of mental prayer. Interior prayer, fed by the Bible and the Liturgy, moves more or less steadily towards greater simplicity and freedom in the spiritual life. In no part of that life do we realize more vividly the glorious liberty of the sons of God. It is a commonplace of ascetic theology that the methodical discipline of discursive meditation, though it will never be wholly abandoned, may and often does lead into a more contemplative type of prayer, which dispenses with the formal pattern and "discourse" of meditation. It is difficult to describe this advance and the language of spiritual writers sometimes suggests that the process is more stereotyped than it actually is. The difficulty is caused by the almost limitless variations in what is an intensely personal experience. All these variations, however, do lead in the same direction, towards a greater freedom. So the necessary complement to liturgical prayer, while like the Liturgy it builds up the priest's soul on the strong and solid foundations of revealed truth, gives him an almost unbounded range of spiritual exploration and advance. Even if he continues throughout his life to practise discursive meditation, he will from time to time feel free to modify or to abandon its formal pattern and to wait upon God in that "simple regard" wherein adoration and faith find full and free expression.

With all this the priest will expect to gain an ever-deeper understanding of the Faith. This great grace is given at least as much by prayer as by theological study and the reading of many books. It is in worship that we touch the heart of religion and go through the veil of theological propositions to the living reality. We learn to know, not by description but by acquaintance, our setting in the mystical Body of Christ. The interlocking of dogmatic truth becomes plain not simply as a rational system for a merely intellectual satisfaction but as an integrated way of life, an experience of the order of redemption and grace in the deep levels of our being. How there may be a real joy and peace in believing and at the same time a broken and a contrite heart; how grace and free will, law and liberty, activity and what the French call *abandon* can exist together in fruitful harmony; how zeal in prayer is not withered by aridity and the absence of conscious feelings of pleasure or solace: all this the priest learns progressively through his prayer. It is one thing to accept with the mind the dogmatic definition of the doctrine of the Trinity or of the Two Natures; it is another to discover, as we do in the life of prayer, that these dogmas are light and power for living in charity with God and man. Dogma without prayer is dead, a lifeless framework of formally correct propositions. But "this is the Catholic Faith, that we worship". Only by loving God can we live in him.

2

There are two aspects of that love which call for particular attention in the priest's life of prayer.

The first is intercessory prayer, in which we give practical expression to that love of the brethren which, as the First Epistle of John insists, is the test of the reality of our love of God. The second is that godly sorrow which makes the priest a penitent. Both of these are constant aids in maintaining vitality and freshness in the endless adventure of the prayer life.

There is a paradox about intercessory prayer. Many find intercession the kind of prayer that comes most easily and naturally to them. Yet intercession presents well-known problems, both theoretical and practical, some common to all petitionary prayer, some peculiar to prayer for other people. On what grounds is it right and necessary to ask God, who *ex hypothesi* is all-knowing, all-wise, and all-loving, to confer benefits on others? Or, to put the question more bluntly, does intercession imply either naïve presumption on our part or a very defective idea of God? If intercession is to take its rightful place in the priest's spiritual life, its theological grounds need to be understood. For, in fact, intercession is of the very substance of priesthood.

There are two positive principles of Christian theology which logically require the practice of intercession.

The first principle is expressed in the closely related doctrines of the Holy Spirit and the mystical Body of Christ. To be a Christian is to partake of the fellowship of the Holy Spirit and every Christian is a co-operator with the Spirit, who is the soul of the Church, the giver of life, and the source of all spiritual gifts. This co-operation is active; it is not merely a passive reception of some external force but calls for a positive response of the will. Next, this co-operation is with the Spirit in the Body of Christ. It may be pictured as vertical—man working with God—and horizontal—man working for man. If, therefore, the action of God upon man is so ordered by the divine will that men are called into some real, though limited, co-operation with him, it follows that the conferring of benefits by God upon men will be in some measure conditioned by the acts and wills of men. God will confer benefits upon A both directly— since God's sovereign freedom is not bound in any way— and indirectly, through the acts and prayers of B.

Let us assume that B is a Christian and understands his Christian privilege and responsibility. He will, both by prayers and goods works, seek to exercise his function as a co-operator with God towards A.

The doctrine of the mystical Body leads to the same conclusion. We are members one of another and each member has a contribution to make to the welfare of the whole. It is obvious that this applies to prayer as well as to works. For it is absurd to suppose that in prayer we automatically shut off the rest of life and, in particular, our concern for other people. Thus it is both as co-operating with the immanent activity of the Spirit and also in the mutual service of membership in Christ's Body that we are bound to the duty of intercession.

The second principle is to be seen in the truth that the Christian life is, in essence, the manifestation of charity. The perfection of God is his charity and that charity is the standard set for the Christian by Jesus Christ in the Sermon on the Mount. Both in good works and in prayer the Christian must manifest charity. By intercessory prayer in the name of Christ and in the fellowship of the Spirit he aligns himself with the operation of the divine charity. His ontological status as a partaker of the Holy Ghost and as a member of the Body of Christ carries with it a moral obligation of charity in thought, word, and deed.

From this point of view it is clear that quantitative

ideas—so much intercession, so much result—are irrelevant and absurd. We pray in faith. We recognize the infinite complexity of the Spirit's action. We do not make the ridiculous demand that this supernatural activity shall be tested by the simple mechanics of the penny-in-the-slot machine. Above all, we see our intercessory prayer not as some magic, whereby we may manipulate supernatural forces for ends that seem to us desirable, but as submission to the energy of God the Holy Spirit, active within the redeemed community of Christ's people.

When we consider the practical questions raised by intercessory prayer, the special problem is the limitless range and complexity of human needs. How are we to deal with the, at first sight paralysing, fact that it is humanly impossible to cover the ground when we tackle the work of intercession?

We may begin by recalling the parable of the Good Samaritan. His good work was that which was called for by his personal contact with a man in need as he went about his ordinary business. He did not spend all his days vainly seeking out wounded men on every lonely road in Palestine. So with our intercessions; the first claim upon us is the needs that present themselves in the ordinary contacts of daily life.

Yet even so, as we widen our field of interest with the years, we find that the demands on our prayers are many and various and tend to become more so. We must, therefore, be businesslike and recognize the need of some order and system in the work of intercession. A system based on the week, allotting to each day one or two main topics, is a useful device. It is possible to break up the subject or subjects for the day and allot one part to each of our liturgical acts of worship, as well as to have a separate time, in addition to the Eucharist and the offices. It should be remembered that in the prayer for the Church at the Eucharist we have the central focus of intercession and one that is integrated with the main act of sacrifice and worship.

Recognition of our dependence upon the Holy Spirit is the safeguard against the vain notion that when we intercede we are reminding God of what he does not know or fails to remember. It is a safeguard also against the kind of nervous scrupulosity that sometimes lurks in elaborately detailed schemes of intercession, a half-conscious fear that if we do not mention every detail it will escape God's notice. These arithmetical ideas must be banished. Individually, we are members of the Body, not the whole Body; and all our deficiencies, where they are not just negligence and sloth, are swallowed up in the Holy Spirit's all-comprehending activity.

Clear conviction on the *rationale* of intercession is of especial importance for the priest. Priesthood is essentially mediatory; the priest is one who speaks for God to men and for men to God. In the full sense of the term, priesthood belongs only to the God-man, Jesus Christ, but in the divine economy of the Body of Christ there is a derived and dependent priesthood of the Church and a derived and dependent priesthood of the apostolic ministry. For we live "in Christ", and Christ's priesthood is operative through the corporate priesthood of the redeemed and through the ministerial priesthood of bishops and presbyters. The priest, therefore, is essentially an intercessor, and his intercessory functions must appear both in his work and in his prayer. In work, in suffering, in prayer he is to be one with Christ the mediator, whose spokesman and representative he is.

To give due expression to this fundamental truth means a good deal more than a few vocal prayers a day. Such prayers, good and necessary as they are, are but one fruit of that mediatorial life which is the true character of priesthood. Those whom we revere as models of priesthood, a Fr Benson, a Fr Wainwright, a Curé d'Ars, are supremely those who *lived* for their people, whose lives were intercessory lives, and who as they stood each morning at the altar were doing something that was of a piece with what was to follow throughout their working day. At the altar and in the confessional they brought God to men and men to God; so too in the streets and lanes and houses of their parishes and in the privacy of their interior prayer. We must have our intercession lists, our daily times for direct intercessory petitions, our varying techniques and methods for presenting the needs of others to God, when we kneel down in our churches or our homes and concentrate attention on this work. But all this is fruit not root. It is but a part of a larger whole, that life of mediation to which those whom Christ makes his ministers are committed by their ordination.

A parish priest, as he visits a community of enclosed religious, and takes part in the unbroken intercession maintained throughout the day in the chapel, may be conscious of a pang of longing. If only he had more time for this holy work! But there are diversities of gifts and operations. No doubt he may be brought by such an experience to a real contrition for failure to use the time he has or could have. Yet he must not think himself debarred by his laborious days and endless business from a truly intercessory life, as truly intercessory as the ceaseless prayer of the convent chapel. All depends on how he regards his work. If he does it as priestly work, intercessory and mediatorial in its very nature; if he often renews his intention to offer it as such; then he is truly entering into the high privilege of the intercessor and truly sharing the life of him who ever liveth to make intercession for us.

3

We love God by being intercessors. We love him also by being penitents. The element of discipline in the spiritual life is not merely the observance of certain rules by which we safeguard the order and regularity of our spiritual exercises. The man of God has to be disciplined at a deeper level, by a life of what spiritual writers call mortification. That "continual mortifying of our corrupt affections" for which we pray in the Easter Even Collect goes side by side with the life of prayer. As Fr Augustine Baker puts it in *Holy Wisdom*, "in those two duties of mortification and prayer all good is comprehended; for by the exercise of mortification those two general most deadly enemies of our souls, self-love and pride, are combated and subdued, to wit, by the means of those two fundamental virtues of divine charity and humility".

Mortification has often been misunderstood, by some who have sought to practise it as well as by those who have thought it meant salvation by works and have therefore scorned it as a papistical corruption of the Gospel. It has been misunderstood when it has been confused with the superstitious fancy that we are displeasing to God unless we do a sufficient number of unpleasant things, especially in the way of bodily austerities. The truth is that mortification may, or may not, carry with it some form of bodily austerity, which is never an end in itself but a means whereby we may become pure in heart; and, secondly, that mortification is the way in which a genuine contrition and a genuine purpose of amendment express themselves. For by mortification we take penitence out of the sphere of sorrowful regrets and painful emotions and make it a realistic response to God not only with our lips (or our feelings) but in our lives. Prayer without mortification is in danger of becoming but a form of pietistic self-indulgence, and a highly dangerous one.

Penitence is a constructive and positive element in the spiritual life, wholly different from mere remorse or obsessions of guilt. It has its negative aspect in renunciation of evil, sorrow for sin, avoidance of occasions of sin, and sometimes sharp and stern treatment of desires, impulses, and habits, even when they are not sinful in themselves. This, however, is but the clearing of the ground for the positively fruitful work of penitence, that is to say for the graces of renewed vision, reawakened wonder and gratitude, fresh longing for God and his holiness, and, as a result, a practical endeavour after singlemindedness, that purity of heart without which we shall not see God. The life of mortification is the day-to-day actualization, by the power of the Holy Spirit, of this twofold aim, the cleansing of the soul and the redirection of its energies. Both are equally necessary; for we know what happens to the soul that is swept and garnished and then left in that bare and useless vacuity.

The priest's spiritual life will, therefore, be the life of a penitent, a warfare not merely *against* "the most deadly enemies of our soul, self-love and pride" but also *for* "those two fundamental Christian virtues of divine charity and humility". To this end he will have both his over-all strategy and his day-to-day tactics.

The strategical plan is, in the main, nothing else but that pattern of God-centred living which we have tried to sketch in outline and to which we must now add regular self-examination and confession. For the priest this ought to include sacramental confession at certain times. The Church provides us with the sacrament of penance primarily as a means of reconciliation for those who by grave sin have cut themselves off from the supernatural life of the redeemed. But the divine mercy has permitted a wider use of sacramental confession and absolution, and this sacrament has come to be a regular component of the spiritual life, whether or not there is mortal sin on the conscience. The privilege of going to confession at regular intervals and receiving the benefit of absolution together with ghostly counsel and advice has proved of untold value. Since the upheaval of the sixteenth century we have to recognize differences of opinion and practice among Anglicans on the question of sacramental confession and especially on the question whether we "must" go to confession. This is not the place to discuss matters of jurisdiction. Here we are concerned with spiritual goods and verifiable facts of the spiritual life. Seen from this angle, sacramental confession commends itself beyond doubt to those who use it; and no priest can afford to make it other than a matter of conscience, whether he will hearken or whether he will forbear. As he may at any time be called upon to hear confessions and give absolution, he has an added responsibility in this matter; for how can he be content to exercise this ministry, if he never experiences its benefits for his own soul?

Sacramental confession, however, is but a part of the penitential life. The priest cannot be a penitent only when he is preparing for confession. He needs constant vigilance against the insidious attacks of self-love in its manifold forms; he needs, too, constant inward renewal by meditation on the sacred humanity of Jesus Christ as he reads the gospels, constant submission to the godly motions of the Spirit as he enters daily into the liturgical worship of the Body of Christ. Indeed, his whole prayer life is, from one point of view, an exercise in mortification and penitence. Special penitential devotions, in Lent or in preparation for receiving the sacraments, are but occasions of heightened attention, those focal points of concentration without which our frail human nature is only too ready to slump and sag to a low level of listless routine.

These principles must penetrate the priest's daily behaviour and be embodied in the multitude of little things which are the raw material of sanctification. His "Lord, I am not worthy" as he prepares to receive Holy Communion must not be forgotten as he deals with the tiresome caller or the dreary committee. The vision of the Lord's selfless obedience and radiant charity which he saw in his morning meditation must not be forgotten as the day passes in a constant procession of exhausting demands upon his energy, his patience, and his resource. And when he does relax, he has still to be watchful against the demons of sensuality and sloth, ready to take advantage of his fatigue, just as in his busy hours he must guard against temptations to anger, pride, or envy. So and no otherwise the warfare is waged, so the watch must be kept; and there is no road to victory save that of prayer and mortification.

In two ways the priest can help himself. They are familiar, but a brief reminder of them may not be out of place. The first is a rule of life, which every priest must make for himself and from time to time revise. The second is the deliberate cultivation of that recollectedness which is sometimes called "the practice of the presence of God" in Brother Lawrence's phrase. That humility which lies at the the heart of the mortified and penitent priest depends most of all on a habitual reference to, and dependence upon, the Holy Spirit. No illuminist extravagances must be allowed to blind us to the reality of the Spirit's aid and the power of this deliberately willed (not "felt") submission to his control as we meet the changing contingencies of daily life. We shall continue to make mistakes and we shall not be miraculously exempt from the possibility of sin. What we shall find is a constant check upon our wilfulness and our egoism, a constant reminder of our Example, a constant inflow of power to put away temptation, a constant reinforcement of our good desires. And we shall grow in thankfulness, a very great grace, and the most potent of aids to advance in the interior life.